W9-BVC-256

SEWING TO SELL

The Beginner's Guide to Starting a Craft Business

Bonus—16 Starter Projects • How to Sell Locally & Online

Virginia Lindsay

WITHDRAWN

Tribal Library
Saginaw Chippewa Indian Tribe
7070 E. Broadway
Mt. Pleasant MI 48858

stashBOOKS®

an imprint of C&T Publishing

Text and Photography copyright © 2014 by Virginia Lindsay

Photography and Artwork copyright © 2014 by C&T Publishing, Inc.

Publisher: Amy Marson

Creative Director: Gailen Runge

Art Director/Book Designer: Kristy Zacharias

Editors: Lynn Koolish and Lee Jonsson

Technical Editors: Alison M. Schmidt and Mary E. Flynn

Page Layout Artist: Katie McIntosh

Production Coordinator: Jenny Davis

Production Editor: Alice Mace Nakanishi

Illustrator: Valyrie Gillum

Photo Assistant: Mary Peyton Peppo

Styled photos by Nissa Brehmer and instructional photos by
Diane Pedersen, unless otherwise noted

Published by Stash Books, an imprint of C&T Publishing, Inc., P.O. Box 1456,
Lafayette, CA 94549

All rights reserved. No part of this work covered by the copyright hereon
may be used in any form or reproduced by any means—graphic, electronic,
or mechanical, including photocopying, recording, taping, or information
storage and retrieval systems—without written permission from the
publisher. Note: The designs in this book may be used to make items for
personal use or for sale without limitations.

Attention Copy Shops: Please note the following exception—publisher and
author give permission to photocopy pattern pullout pages P1 and P2 for
personal use only.

Attention Teachers: C&T Publishing, Inc., encourages you to use this book
as a text for teaching. Contact us at 800-284-1114 or ctpub.com for lesson
plans and information about the C&T Creative Troupe.

We take great care to ensure that the information included in our products
is accurate and presented in good faith, but no warranty is provided nor
are results guaranteed. Having no control over the choices of materials or
procedures used, neither the author nor C&T Publishing, Inc., shall have
any liability to any person or entity with respect to any loss or damage
caused directly or indirectly by the information contained in this book.
For your convenience, we post an up-to-date listing of corrections on our
website (ctpub.com). If a correction is not already noted, please contact
our customer service department at ctinfo@ctpub.com or at P.O. Box 1456,
Lafayette, CA 94549.

Trademark (™) and registered trademark (®) names are used throughout
this book. Rather than use the symbols with every occurrence of a
trademark or registered trademark name, we are using the names only in
the editorial fashion and to the benefit of the owner, with no intention of
infringement.

Library of Congress Cataloging-in-Publication Data

Lindsay, Virginia Keleher, 1975-

Sewing to sell : the beginner's guide to starting a craft business : bonus,
16 starter projects : how to sell locally & online / Virginia Lindsay.

    pages cm

Includes bibliographical references.

ISBN 978-1-60705-903-5 (soft cover)

1. Handicraft industries--Management--Handbooks, manuals, etc.
2. Home-based businesses--Management--Handbooks, manuals, etc.
3. Small business--Management--Handbooks, manuals, etc. 4. Selling--
Handbooks, manuals, etc. I. Title.

HD9999.H363L56 2014

646.2068--dc23

                            2014013070

Printed in China

10 9 8 7 6 5 4 3 2 1

Dedication

This book is dedicated to my husband, Travis Lindsay. His confidence in my ability to create has given me the perspective that I can accomplish anything. And to my four children—Elsie, Anne, Calvin, and Marion—who inspire me every day.

Acknowledgments

Thank you so much to C&T Publishing for making this book possible and, in particular, Lynn Koolish, Roxane Cerda, and the rest of the team who worked on this book with me.

Thank you to my mom for her continued support and taking me to the craft store over and over again when I was a kid.

Thank you to my kind and thoughtful child-caregivers, Carly Deel and Donna McGuire. It felt wonderful to have my kids well cared for while I was working on this book.

Thank you to my good friend Amy Frank for letting me pick her sewing brain over and over again and for sending me her beautiful Blessing Band for support and inspiration.

Thank you so much to my sister-in-law and wonderful friend Jennifer Stein. Her fantastic photography is featured in this book. I can always count on Jen for friendship and support.

Thank you to my sewing friends Amy Dunn and Vanessa Hewell for always being there to talk sewing and to share their wisdom and photos for the book.

Thank you to Jessica Rider, Monica Donohue, and Candace Todd for letting me interview them and answering all my nosy questions!

Thank you to Jessica Fincham for sharing her beautiful sewing studio photos.

Thank you to Pam Thompson, Jen Primack, Debbie Pearson, Debra Cooper, and Jennifer Johnson for sharing photos of their beautiful handmade work.

Thank you to Art Gallery Fabrics, Dear Stella, Dritz, Monaluna, Fairfield, FreeSpirit Fabrics, Moda, Robert Kaufman Fabrics, Timeless Treasures, and The Warm Company.

CONTENTS

Projects

Appendix   143

INTRODUCTION

The fun of sewing, as with many creative endeavors, is creating delightful things that are beautifully designed and made with fabrics you love. For many of you, sewing hooks you and becomes a passion. You see wonderful fabrics and have to buy them. Then, of course, you want to try new techniques and ideas to use that fabulous fabric. You stay up late because you just have to finish that last seam and admire your completed work.

This enchantment with sewing can become a useful and valuable asset. Whether you sew curtains and pillows or pinafores and elegant evening bags, being able to sew is a skill that sets you apart. If you can sew, you can create something useful *and* beautiful. Many of our grandmothers sewed out of necessity. Most women had to be able to do their own mending and hemming. They made most of their children's clothes and many of their own. They sewed tablecloths and pillowcases. They sewed aprons and quilts. Their skills were taken for granted, and sewing was often a chore along with the cooking and cleaning. Now, sewing is a choice that we make because we are drawn to create with fabric.

I love the nostalgia of sewing. It makes me feel connected to the past and to all those ladies who used to spend so much time with their needle and thread. I love how handmade things have a history and a personal connection.

This personal connection is missing when you buy something that was made in an anonymous factory. This human touch and personal connection is why so many people are coming back to sewing and looking to buy handmade goods.

Making the leap from sewing for personal use to sewing as a professional can be a bit intimidating, and it's only natural to feel a bit daunted. Yes, you will need to work hard on your skills and make sure your work is well made. You cannot go from just learning to sew to opening a shop, but you also don't have to be an expert sewist with twenty years of sewing experience either. Most likely, it is not your sewing skills that are holding you back, but rather your concerns about running a business and creating something that is worth buying.

The purpose of this book is to get you off the sidelines and start sewing your way to a job that you will truly enjoy. The informational chapters will give you all the resources you need to begin on the right foot. This book also includes sixteen sewing projects that you have permission to use so that you have a collection of go-to items to stock up your new shop. (This is not the case for all projects in books. For more information on copyrights and permissions, see Using Sewing Patterns to Get Started, page 10.) I imagine you will change my patterns and rework them to suit your own creative strengths, and I encourage you to do so! These patterns will be a great place for you to begin and then look at again when your shop needs something new and fresh.

As a special bonus, each group of projects gives you additional information on packaging, photographing your work for online sales, and promotional ideas.

Finally, I hope this book convinces you that you deserve to love your job and that you *can* make money doing something you love. Whether you create iPad covers or elaborate quilts, sewing to sell is a worthwhile and satisfying endeavor. As with all jobs, some parts you will really like and other parts will be a challenge for you to enjoy. But treating yourself like a professional, with a boss who demands hard work and expects the best (yes, that boss is you), will help you to become a well-rounded and successful seller of your own handmade goods.

FINDING YOUR SEWING STYLE

We all have our specific likes and dislikes—certain colors, patterns, textures, and combinations that we find attractive. Your own specific style is what makes you unique. I am not talking about cutting-edge, wild, truly original style here (although if you have it, go for it), but instead, being true to what appeals to you.

Authenticity

It can be hard to put a specific name to your personal style, and trying to do so can artificially constrain you. Are you a romantic because you like ruffles? What if you like ruffles and bright colors? What if you like ruffles, bright colors, and only organic fabrics? What's important is that you know what you like and what you want to make. Making what *you* think is beautiful and useful is a surefire way to create a successful business—authenticity matters so much in a handmade business.

Tip

TRY THIS: Many people struggle to get a feel for their own unique look. It can feel like a crisis in decision making or self-confidence. A great way to get a feel for your own style is to gather together prints, colors, shapes, and textures that appeal to you. Buy a corkboard or a large poster board. Pin or tape up pictures, ribbons, colors, and fabric scraps that you like, and anything else that you think is "you." Keep this up in your sewing room to help you stay focused and keep yourself in touch with your own likes and style preferences.

This authenticity and sense of personal style will give your work a cohesive look and will help you sell your work to your target group of customers who share your aesthetic. Although I try to think about what my customer may want to buy, it is always balanced by what I would want to make for myself. Through some trial and error, you can easily find a happy place that appeals to both you and your customers without sacrificing your personal sense of style.

This beautiful room is the studio of fiber artist Debra Cooper. She uses an inspiration board to keep her work fresh and authentic to her own style.

Photo by Debra Cooper

Using Sewing Patterns to Get Started

Working according to your own style strengths is something that comes with time and experience. A great place to start is to sew patterns that you know are thoughtfully designed to be useful and simple to make. It is important to read the fine print so you know if you are allowed to sell what you make from someone else's pattern. Some pattern designers allow sales with a purchase, others ask that you purchase a separate license, and others forbid sales from their patterns. It is important to respect a designer's copyrights when it comes to using their patterns to make items to sell. Make sure you check before you purchase a pattern. If you don't see any specific information on the pattern, contact the pattern maker to ask for permission.

Using a pattern is an easy place to start because you already know that you like the design of the pattern, and you can add your own imprint on the style by your choice of fabrics and perhaps embellishments.

When you have a sense of what your style is, you are ready to move on to deciding who you want to sew for and exactly want you want to sell.

Tip

Why not start here? You have permission to use all of the patterns in this book to make things to sell. Use them, modify them, make them yours, or use them as is.

Interview with Jessica Rider of A Little Gray

Photo by Nick Rider

Jessica Rider is a modern quilter and sewist residing in Cincinnati. Her urban, down-to-earth style appeals to many but is uniquely her own. Not only is Jessica an accomplished quilt designer and president of the Cincinnati Modern Quilt Guild, but she is also a talented designer of children's clothes and has won the popular blog contest Project Run and Play.

Photo by Kristin Timm

Quilt by Jessica Rider of A Little Gray

How would you describe your style?

Modern, bright, and urban/earthy with a sense of humor and a little edge.

Are there certain colors and patterns you like best?

Definitely. I tend to use cool colors along with golds, grays, and blacks. I need my color combos to have an unexpected contrast and not be too sugary sweet. I think patterns that are tone-on-tone or color blends are the most useful for me. I always pick geometrics over florals, but I also love patterns based on other natural inspirations such as wood grain or clouds.

How do you know when something looks good together?

I do a lot of auditioning when it comes to the fabrics I sew with. When I finally realized I don't like using orange and therefore don't need to buy orange fabric for my stash, it was a huge revelation. I've found that if my stash is full of fabrics that are my favorite colors and patterns, it's very likely that a lot of them will work together nicely. So when I put two things next to each other, I usually know immediately if I want to see them sewn together. It's much harder for me to narrow down the options in a combo than it is to find a good match. But that's when I try to use the wisdom of the great Tim Gunn—"edit, edit, edit." A lot of times the simplest combination is the most genius.

Who or what are some of your style influences?

I started quilting when I took a class taught by Heather Jones, who used a book written by Elizabeth Hartman. Both have extremely distinct styles within modern quilting, so I feel like I got an excellent introduction to that movement, as well as the possibilities within it. Heather and I share a love of using solids, and I picked up her obsession with dense straight-line quilting as well. From Elizabeth, I clung to the mixing of prints and the traditional-goes-modern designs. As far as fabric designers, I'm a big fan of Lizzy House. I can't seem to make anything without a little Pearl Bracelet in it.

Name a sewist whose work you like but whose style is different from your own. What about their style appeals to you?

Lately I have really been admiring the work of Camille Roskelley of Bonnie & Camille and Thimble Blossoms. Although the style of her fabric is basically the exact opposite of what I usually go for, I can truly appreciate its beauty, especially the way she uses the fabrics in her sweet vintage quilts. She's a wonderful example of someone who has found great creative success by knowing her style and sticking to it.

(continued)

Where do you find style inspiration?

Everywhere. My city, my family, modern art, bookstores, thrift stores, Instagram, graphics in ads, my Modern Quilt Guild, pop music, TV and movies, buildings, fashion, and even the zoo. I try not to limit the number of real-life sources I might find inspiration from, and I usually have a notepad with me to jot or doodle ideas. At the same time, I do like to take breaks from the constant flow of inspiration on the Internet. (Don't tell anyone, but I'm a terrible blog reader.) If you tried to make every single sewing fad (or pin) out there, it would be impossible to truly cultivate a style.

I should also mention that I'm fortunate enough to work part time in a gorgeous modern fabric shop, Sewn Studio in Cincinnati. I'm surrounded by beautiful fabric and passionate sewists on a regular basis. That is amazingly inspiring.

Photo by Jessica Rider

Do you have an inspiration/style board in your sewing room?

Nope. I think by the time I'm in the sewing room, inspiration is already there and it's time to get busy. (With little kids, time in that sacred room is valuable.) What I do have is several gifted mini quilts on the wall that mean a lot to me, including ones from my mom and grandmother. They remind me that sewing and making is in my heritage and that I am lucky to have so many friends and family that share this passion.

Do you find yourself influenced by trends, or do you just do your own thing stylewise?

A little of both. I'm not against trends at all, but I'm rebellious enough that I have to find a way to do a trend as no one else is doing it. I think that if you can join in some of the fun things going on in the sewing community while still standing out and making it your own, that is a sure sign of signature style. I just try to also step back on occasion and make something out in left field, something no one else is even thinking about. I really like to work within a certain creative challenge and see what I can come up with, for example, designing a very modern quilt starting with a traditional block, or designing a child's outfit inspired by an artsy movie. Sometimes giving your creativity some parameters is what helps it grow the most.

Jessica Rider

IDENTIFYING YOUR CUSTOMERS

Photo by Virginia Lindsay

Try to focus on a specific customer; for example, I made this art caddy specifically for little boys.

Now for the question of whom you are going to sew for. At home, when you are sewing for yourself, you can sew whatever you like. One day you may feel like sewing a pretty pink baby blanket, and the next you are making your boyfriend a camouflage canvas wallet. Switching projects around is great for improving your skills and flexing those creative muscles. My sewing room is full of projects from all sorts of different moods and interests. Switching it up is wonderful when you are sewing as a hobby, but when you want to make the transition to selling your creations as a profession, you need to make some clear decisions and focus on a specific group of people to sew for. Then follow your sense of style (see Finding Your Sewing Style, page 8) to give your work a cohesive and professional look.

Be Selective

It's unrealistic to try to please everyone, and it's a bad strategy for success. Trying to sew something for everyone will only confuse your shopper and leave you feeling as though you can't please anyone. You don't want to have something for baby right next to a masculine journal cover because this will turn away both shoppers.

When friends and neighbors found out that I was sewing professionally, the suggestions became a bit overwhelming. I have been told to sew everything from slipcovers and matchbox car wallets to tutus and appliance covers. Once I had an acquaintance describe to me in detail a bag she thought I should sew that could hold all her child's sports equipment. The ideas are endless and sometimes can lead to wonderful potential projects, but knowing which are valuable and which are simply distracting can be a challenge. This is where choosing a specific customer will direct you and ease your decision making.

I sew mostly items for babies and children because I enjoy sewing bright and colorful accessories and pillows for them. I also include a few mom items because I know the mothers of these children will be the shoppers. Sewing for kids was a natural place for me to land because I have four kids.

Of course, this is not to say that if you have kids, you need to choose sewing for kids. A good friend of mine has four little kids too but sews clutches, cuffs, and purses for women. She seems to know what will look great and makes a stylish statement by choosing funky fabrics and great design. When I try to sew fashion accessories for women, I am indecisive and a little frustrated. Although I admire fashion and love to shop, I realize my own shortcomings in regard to sewing women's fashions myself. I am much more interested and comfortable sewing for kids.

There are many special niches, such as travel, wedding accessories, electronics covers, and pets. Three good possibilities with many opportunities are sewing for children, sewing fashion accessories, and sewing for the home. Trying to find which is best for you is as simple as deciding what group you like to sew for. Are you really good at mixing bold fabrics for fashion accessories? Do you love to create soft blankets for babies? Is it fun for you to make trendy bags for teenagers? Do you love to make pillows to brighten home decor? Or do you want to sew other things? Be sure to evaluate your own strengths and interests and not what someone else tells you is best for sales.

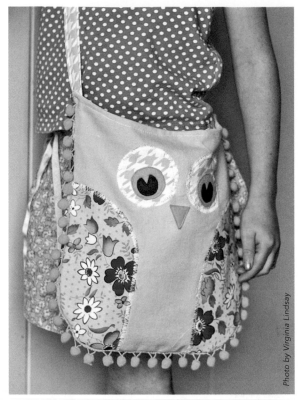

Photo by Virginia Lindsay

These owl bags are best sellers for my company, Gingercake, and me—I make them specifically for kids.

Photo by Virginia Lindsay

These organizers were created specifically as travel accessories for my online shop.

SEWING FOR KIDS AND BABIES

Children are a huge market for handmade goods. Buyers are always looking for gifts and accessories for kids. There is something special and wholesome about spending your money on a gift for a child that will be treasured for its handmade appeal. Fabrics for kids are bright and fun, with all sorts of themes and textures. You can specialize in children's bedding, wardrobe, toys, or accessories. Handmade dolls and plush toys are a popular specialty.

Simple skirts and peasant blouses are currently trendy, but you need to stay on top of what's in style.

Sewing for babies is practically a whole category of its own. Some people love to sew itty-bitty things for little ones. Babies need so many basics that are easy to make, including bibs, burp cloths, gowns, bedding, hats, swaddle blankets, and slings.

Photo by Jen Primack

Photo by Virginia Lindsay

(*Left*) I love it when sewists use the thrift store to find hand-me-down T-shirts to make cute skirts and dresses. Upcycled dress made by Jen Primack of upcycleddesign.etsy.com. (*Right*) Bibs made by Virginia Lindsay

SEWING FASHION ACCESSORIES

Every woman needs a little handmade splash to liven up her style. If fashion accessories are your interest, you should be able to have lots of fun putting together your line of handmade items. The only problem you may have is limiting your selection. The most successful sewists usually stick to one area of fashion accessories—for example, a line of shoulder bags, wallets, and clutches. Another area may be scarves, cuffs, and belts.

A group of accessories somewhere between fashion and home are the sewing projects for electronics. These are really popular right now, and buyers seem to love a handmade cover to soften the look of their latest gadget. If you find a great piece you love to sew and it sells well in fashion accessories, you can build a whole line of handmade goods around that piece and have a great look to your shop.

This group of clutches and totes, by Amy Frank of Mindfully Made Studios, looks great together and will attract shoppers who are looking to accessorize!

Photo by Amy Dunn

Made by Amy Dunn of pinkedfabrics.etsy.com

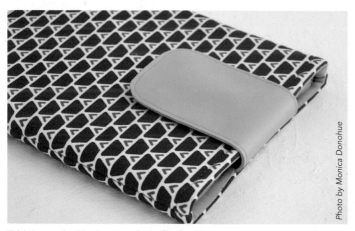

Photo by Monica Donohue

Tablet cover by Monica Donohue of little-pigeon.com

Sewing for Fundraising

Many sewists want to use their talents to sew specifically for a fundraising effort. It's important to focus your efforts in the same way as if you were sewing for profit. Whether you are sewing for a local church festival or a cancer society, feeling passionate about what you are sewing is still important. Think about choosing appropriate fabrics and items that might relate to what you are trying to accomplish.

Often, online sellers choose to donate a percentage of their sales to online charities. This is a great way to contribute to your community. It can also help to give you a special direction and focus, and it lets your customers know what you really care about.

Photo by Pam Thompson

Tote by Pam Thompson of helpandhold.com; Pam donates 10% of her profits to a local women's shelter in Philadelphia.

SEWING FOR THE HOME

Sewing for the home is the perfect category for people who love to decorate. It's for people who know how to add a pop of color and how to make a boring chair look cozy and welcoming with a handmade pillow or lap quilt. Home-decorating styles are as different and interesting as individual personalities. Some basic categories of home decorating are modern, shabby chic, eclectic, and traditional. You can also choose to sew for the kitchen by making aprons, napkins, tablecloths, potholders, and kitchen towels.

Some shops are entirely devoted to throw pillows. Pillows are a fun and creative way to add a special handmade look to your home at little cost. Creating pillow covers takes a special skill for finding beautiful fabrics and having an eye for home decor.

Sewing for the home is an excellent market for wedding and special occasion gifts. Specializing in thoughtful handmade throws; simple, colorful quilts; or gorgeous, fancy table linens is a smart way to use your skills to make and sell something beautiful. Home accessories are a great way to use vintage fabric too. This is a fun way to add nostalgic and funky interest to home decorating.

Apron by Debbie Pearson of creativechics.etsy.com

Potholders by Virginia Lindsay

ESSENTIAL EQUIPMENT

Your Sewing Machine

If your sewing studio is a movie, then your sewing machine is your superstar. My first advice is to take good care of your star—either learn how to clean and oil it yourself or take it regularly to a repair shop that will keep it in good shape for you. You need to have a working machine that you like and feel comfortable using.

I am not here to recommend that you buy a new sewing machine unless you are still using a cheap machine from a big box store, maybe the one you learned on. You are not going to

be able to get quality, reliability, and durability with a casual, light-duty machine. Those basic machines are fine for learning and sewing basic things, but you can't sew the volume needed to be a professional on a beginner's machine. You need a sturdy, reliable machine to handle the volume of projects that you have in your future.

You don't need a fancy machine. Just make sure your machine has the following features:

- Adjustable stitch length or at least three different lengths
- Adjustable zigzag or at least three widths of zigzag stitch
- A way to make good buttonholes

The basic requirements listed above are for sewing with cotton fabrics. If you are going to sew on knit fabrics, you will also need to use some stitches that allow for stretch. Most basic sewing machines include these options and many more that you may never use. A good machine should also easily handle thicker fabrics such as canvas and even leather with the proper needles.

Photo by Virginia Lindsay

My machine is a classic workhorse.

Photo by Jennifer Stein of jennifersteinphoto.com

MACHINE ACCESSORIES

The magic of using the correct sewing machine accessories is truly wonderful. I have only the basic accessories, and I find that I can get all my sewing accomplished as long as I use the correct needle and presser foot. I always have plenty of size 14/90 microtex needles so that I can use a new needle whenever I am starting a new big project. A good rule might be to change your needle every two or three bobbin changes. A new needle keeps your stitches looking pretty. I also have a stash of 100/16 denim needles that I use when I am sewing through thick layers and heavy fabrics.

The other needles that I always have on hand are ball-point needles for sewing knits. These needles are designed to glide between the loops of a knit fabric without disturbing the fibers that make up the fabric and either skipping or causing runs.

The other important machine accessory is the proper presser foot. I use three feet regularly, but many other feet can be used to make your sewing creations look more professional and make your job a lot easier.

- **STANDARD PRESSER FOOT** This is the foot that I use for basic sewing. I can use it for both straight and zigzag stitching. This foot is standard and you can get almost all of your sewing done with this foot alone.

- **¼″ OR PATCHWORK FOOT** This foot gives you a perfect ¼″ seam allowance. It also provides good control for topstitching and patchwork piecing.

- **ZIPPER FOOT** If you are going to install a zipper, this foot is a must. It makes sewing zippers a breeze because you can get close to those teeth without losing sight of your needle or breaking it.

The Value of a Walking Foot

A walking foot is a staple for many sewists because it assists in sewing together layers, which can often slip and move under a regular presser foot.

My good friend Amy Dunn is a talented sewist of patchwork and all things pretty. I asked her about her walking foot, and she said, "A walking foot is an invaluable tool for any sewist, not just quilters. I'm not a quilter and I often use a walking foot to keep layers from shifting—anytime you have more than two layers of fabric you benefit from using a walking foot. If you have layers of fabric and batting or thick interfacing, it is a must. I also use it for topstitching—your stitches will be more even and your machine won't strain as much. If you don't have a walking foot, go get one."

Photos courtesy of Bernina USA

Walking foot

THREAD

Always buy the best thread you can find. I usually use Coats & Clark or Gütermann. Both work well for me, and although not the cheapest, they are reasonably priced. It's important to use good-quality thread with a minimum of loose fibers because those fibers can eventually ruin your tension discs. Poor-quality thread also results in weak seams. I usually have cream, white, and black thread on hand.

My favorite trick is clear thread, which is sometimes called invisible thread. You don't want to use it all the time because it can be a little tricky to use, but you can use it when you don't have a thread that matches your fabrics. I recommend Superior Threads MonoPoly in smoke for dark fabrics and clear for light fabrics. The thread is polyester, so it doesn't get brittle, as nylon thread can, and you can iron it without worrying about melting it.

CUTTING TOOLS

First, you must have a nice, sharp pair of fabric scissors that are used only for cutting fabric. Again, get the best you can afford, but no need to go super fancy. A basic pair of good-quality scissors that you have sharpened regularly should last you a long time and do a great job with your fabrics. A nice pair of pinking shears to trim your open seams is also essential. The primary use of pinking shears is to help prevent fraying, but they are also helpful in trimming curves and for creating a fun, decorative cut. I also recommend a pair of small scissors or snips for cutting and trimming threads.

The other essential cutting tools are the rotary cutter; self-healing cutting mat; and large, clear ruler. If you don't already have these tools, you will be jumping for joy after you make this investment. In fact, I barely even use my scissors now that I am good at using the rotary cutter. Make sure you take good care of the blades and replace them when needed. Get the biggest cutting mat that you can afford so that you can cut yardage with ease. I would recommend at least 18″ × 24″, but 24″ × 36″ is even better.

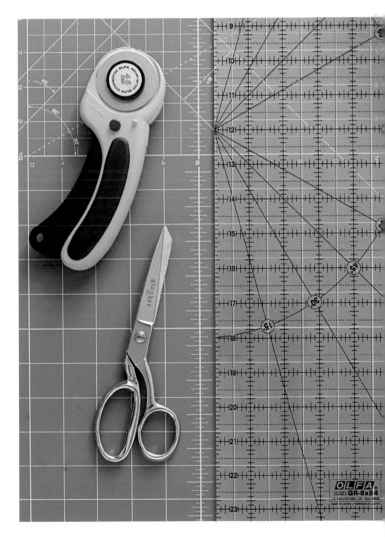

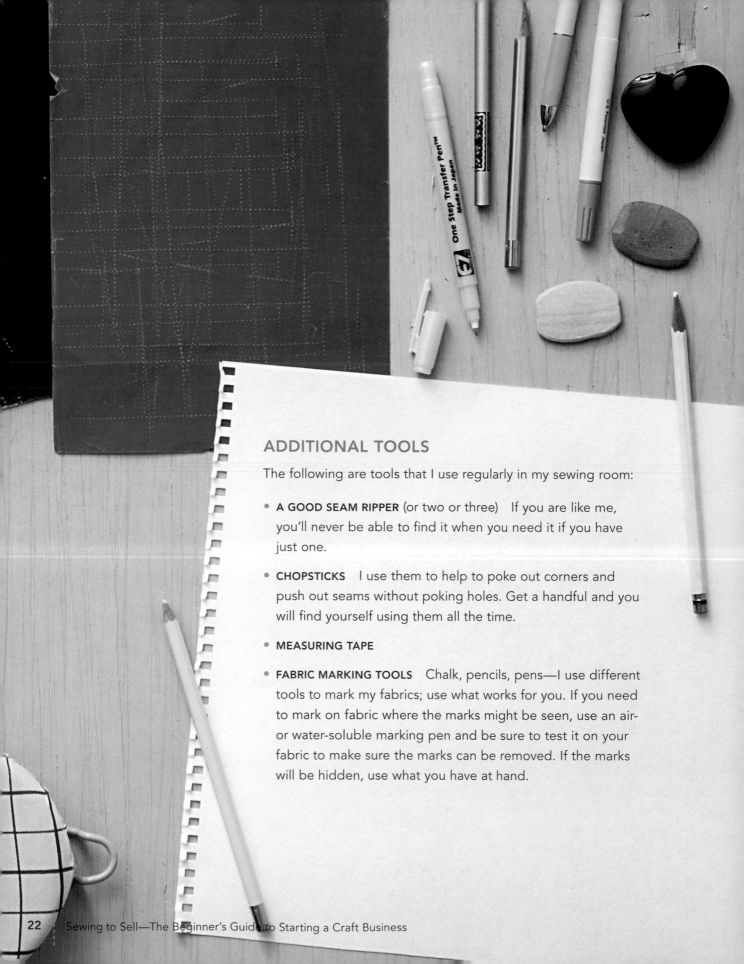

ADDITIONAL TOOLS

The following are tools that I use regularly in my sewing room:

- **A GOOD SEAM RIPPER** (or two or three)   If you are like me, you'll never be able to find it when you need it if you have just one.

- **CHOPSTICKS**   I use them to help to poke out corners and push out seams without poking holes. Get a handful and you will find yourself using them all the time.

- **MEASURING TAPE**

- **FABRIC MARKING TOOLS**   Chalk, pencils, pens—I use different tools to mark my fabrics; use what works for you. If you need to mark on fabric where the marks might be seen, use an air- or water-soluble marking pen and be sure to test it on your fabric to make sure the marks can be removed. If the marks will be hidden, use what you have at hand.

SEWING SPACE

It's important to set up a permanent sewing space. It doesn't need to be an entire room but should be a space where you can have your materials and tools on hand and accessible. Along with a sewing table, you should have a comfortable chair that raises you high enough to use your machine without straining your shoulders and back. You also need a table for fabric cutting and an ironing board and iron.

It can be argued that your ironing station is almost as important as your sewing station. Make sure your iron is in good condition (with a steam setting and nondrip feature) and set up near your sewing machine.

Tip

If you have limited space, a folding table and an ironing board that hangs from the back of a door can be helpful.

Photo by Virginia Lindsay

Cutting area

Serger

A serger is an excellent machine that can be used for all sorts of projects. If you are going to sell clothing, a serger is essential for a professional finish. The overlocking threads finish seams so that they don't fray. But for sewing bags, baby items, pillows, and so on, a serger is not necessary because most of the seams are hidden. It is nice though if you have the extra space and money. Many projects can be made with a serger that would make it worth your investment—napkins, ruffles, and knits are all a breeze with a serger.

Computer

In today's world, you can't operate a successful home sewing business without being able to use your computer. You don't have to be an expert, but you will need to be comfortable with using one. Your computer is your home business life-line and is almost as important as your sewing machine. At the very least, you need a computer to upload pictures and edit them so your creations look their best. At the most, you can use your computer to run an entire handmade business from home. Do some research to find out what programs are available and give yourself time to learn to use them.

When I first bought Photoshop Elements (PSE) to use for photo editing, I had a hard time learning how to use it, even with my husband's help. But now I use it all the time. Not only can I make photos look great, but I also make post-cards, ads, banners, and titles for my sewing projects. PSE is extremely useful once you take the time to learn how to use it.

You'll also want to use your computer for social media such as Facebook, Twitter, Pinterest, blogging, and perhaps setting up an online store. For most of you reading this book, your favorite place to be is sewing away in your sewing room, not working on the computer, right? As with all jobs, you have to take care of the business side of your job on the computer. It's not that bad after you get a system going (see Business Basics, page 144)!

Your computer doesn't have to be cutting-edge technology, but it should be fast enough to upload pictures without long, long waits. It's worth the investment to upgrade if it is holding you back from getting work accomplished.

Camera

Good photos are critical for blogging and selling your work online. If you are just getting started, you'll probably be using a smartphone or a "point-and-shoot" camera. If you're ready for a better camera, your next step is a DSLR (digital single-lens reflex) camera and lens that will give you more control when you are shooting. Unless you know someone who is a knowledgeable photographer, go to a good camera store, explain exactly what you are going to be photographing, and get their advice on the best camera and lens that fit your needs and budget.

Regardless of the type of camera you have, the most important factors in getting good photos to post are lighting (page 43), shooting (page 44), and using photo-editing software (page 44).

With a DSLR camera and the right lens, you can get wonderful close-ups that show the handiwork of your stitches. A better camera will also show the texture of your fabric more vividly and will make your colors look better.

High-quality DSLR camera

The photo on the left was taken with an iPhone, and the photo on the right was taken with a DSLR camera. In this case the differences are minimal, showing that you can use your iPhone camera as long as you have good lighting.

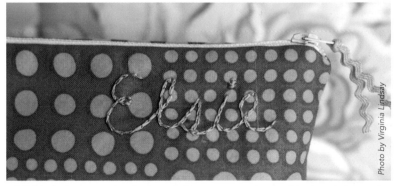

A DSLR with the appropriate lens can help you capture the detail in the stitches and the texture of the fabric, and yet create the pretty *bokeh* (colorful, blurry background) in this photo.

Interview with Vanessa Hewell of LBG Studio

Photo by Vanessa Hewell

Vanessa Hewell is the creator behind LBG Studio. Not only is she talented at sewing and designing, but she also has wonderful style and is a superb photographer. Vanessa is also a friend who has helped me to refine my skills with the camera and the computer.

Tell us about your sewing machine.

I have a Janome DC2010 and have had it for several years now. It is a workhorse. Quite often I find myself sewing through very thick layers, such as canvas plus leather plus quilting cotton. My machine has yet to fail me.

Do you have any machine accessories that you love?

I think my favorite accessory is my walking foot. Although I'm not a quilter, I do use a walking foot often when sewing things with thicker layers, such as bags or wallets, where it is important for things to stay lined up. The walking foot helps keep the layers from shifting, so I end up with a more professional-looking product.

Do you have any tips about thread or needles?

I'm not really particular about thread, but I am picky about needles. I choose better-quality needles that are less likely to break, I use the correct size and type of needle for the fabric and thread I am using, and I replace my machine needle often. Using the proper size needle makes a huge difference while sewing. Because I tend to sew through thick layers, I usually use a size 14 or 16 needle.

What is your favorite tool in the sewing room?

I think it's a tie between my rotary cutter and my Clover Wonder Clips. Using a rotary cutter makes cutting fabric much quicker and much more accurate. I rarely, if ever, use scissors to cut my fabric. The Wonder Clips are perfect for holding together thicker layers of fabric, and they don't distort the fabric as pins do.

Do you recommend a serger? If so, what is your favorite thing to use it for?

Yes. Absolutely. If you plan to do any garment sewing at all, a serger is definitely something to invest in. It speeds up production time, makes garments more durable, and gives a professional look to your creations. I like to use my serger for knits especially because it makes them much easier to work with. A popular serger to consider is the Brother 1034D. It is affordable and reliable, and because of its popularity, you'll find many online resources available, such as tips, videos, and tutorials.

What computer programs do you find most useful for your sewing business?

Photo-editing software is vital if you plan to sell anything online. Professional-looking photos give customers the chance to clearly see the products you are selling. Adobe Photoshop Elements is a great place to start. It is an affordable yet powerful program that can help give your photos polish. You can also use it for graphic design purposes, such as designing your own business cards, blog headers, and more.

Another program I find helpful is GoDaddy Bookkeeping (formerly known as outright.com). It is a subscription book-keeping service that automatically syncs your PayPal and business bank accounts, catego-rizes your income and expenses, and much more. It makes filing business taxes much easier by helping me stay organized with minimal effort on my part.

Do you have a few tips for taking pictures of your sewing?

Find the light. Good lighting is key to taking great photos. Natural light is best, so start by finding a spot that gives you soft, even light. Using a reflector and/or diffuser can help to adjust light to suit your needs.

Keep the background of your photos simple. Avoid having a lot of clutter so that the product you are photographing takes center stage. You can use inexpensive foam core board as a backdrop.

Consider composition carefully. Photographs are often more interesting when the subject is not centered or shot straight on.

Think about staging your products and make use of models or props when possible. This will give customers more information about the product.

Web photo by Vanessa Hewell

Vanessa has written an excellent eBook for photographing your sewn items. It is available in her shop lbgstudio.bigcartel.com.

BUYING AND USING FABRIC

Ah, fabric. For most of us sewists, it is our weakness. It is so pretty and holds so much potential. Ordering online doesn't have the appeal of actually touching the fabric, but the feeling of excitement when you see that thick envelope in your mailbox or the box on your porch is so wonderful that it can turn a terrible day around in a hurry. You open the box and inside is beautifully folded, perfect fabric—and project ideas start coming together in a hurry.

As much as I love getting new fabric, it can be a real challenge for me to make good fabric choices. I cannot tell you how many times I have gone to the store and put a bunch of bolts in my cart only to turn around at the last minute and put 90 percent of it back on the shelf. I get so excited when I see lovely prints that I gather them together, but then I get to the cutting station only to wait in line and realize that I already have shelves full of fabrics and that I really came in only to get a solid red and more fusible interfacing. Drat. My conscience gets the better of me, and the kids groan as we walk back through the store and return most of those pretty prints. I am glad that I have this practical sewist whispering in my ear because not only would I be broke (fabric is not cheap) but my whole house would be full of unused yardage.

I do the same thing with my "shopping cart" online. I load it full of fabrics and then I have to check myself and say, "Do I really need these?" The practical sewist side of me is a drag, but I have learned to appreciate her pragmatic side. The old me bought cute fabric wherever I could find it—a professional sewist needs to make better choices.

Have a Plan

Just as I make a list when I go to the grocery store, I have to have a plan and a shopping list when I buy fabrics. Every sewing project is like a recipe, and you need to have the proper ingredients. For example, if you are planning on making ten boxy pencil cases for a show, do the math to figure out how many yards of fabric you will need for ten cases. Don't buy too much yardage just because you didn't take the time to determine what you need.

Use What You Have

A good friend of mine, Amy Frank, is an avid sewist and teaches sewing classes in Boalsburg, Pennsylvania. Whenever I go to her house and see her sewing room, I see the typical pattern pieces, sewing machine, threads, and scraps

Photo by Virginia Lindsay

of trim. Missing from Amy's studio are shelves full of fabric. A little shocked, I asked where she was hiding all her fabric. It turns out that Amy, who has done tons of shows and sews all the time, buys only the fabric she needs for a show and then uses it all up. She starts by buying 2-yard cuts of fabric that she loves (she doesn't bother searching for sales or bargain shopping). When preparing for her show, she cuts all sorts of different items from her fabric until she has used it up. This includes diaper bags, zipper clutches, and headbands for those small pieces. She doesn't buy new fabric until almost all of that original purchase is gone. This blows my mind. She says, "I get sick of looking at it if I don't just use it up." I have to admit that I have fabric pieces from five years ago that I still haven't used.

Build a Stash

If you don't have the self-control that Amy has, and most of us don't, the nice thing about fabric is that an overpurchasing mistake can still be useful later. So, no need to be too hard on yourself about those impulse buys or changing your mind about colors at the last minute because the fabric will keep nicely on the shelf.

On the bright side, you do need to have basics in your sewing room so that you don't have to repeatedly run to the store and waste your precious sewing time. This is lovingly called your fabric stash. Stash building is a good investment because you will find yourself with plenty of good fabrics to choose from when you are feeling creative. They are the building blocks and contrast fabrics to your more showy and bold fabrics. Because I'm attracted to the big, bold prints, I used to have a shelf full of fabrics that looked great on their own, but they didn't coordinate with anything because I hadn't invested in my fabric stash basics. Finally, I learned that I had to have coordinating smaller prints to support my more showy fabrics.

If you are a quilter or someone who loves to coordinate different prints in their work, your stash basics will include quilting cottons in small prints and patterns, and solids in a variety of colors. These are the supporting characters to your bold prints. A person who sews handbags may have stash fabric of canvas solids, linen, cotton lining fabric, and maybe even leather scraps for embellishments. You may even consider buying a bolt (15–25 yards) of a fabric basic that you use as the foundation for most of your bags.

Having a nice stack of solids is also a great way to accent your sewing, and using solids alone is a really fun way to change things up. Stash building is important for creative confidence, especially if you enjoy coordinating prints. It's fun and satisfying to pull it all together with your stash fabrics, since they will make your main fabric look even better. Supporting prints and colors are key to beautiful combinations, as we will discuss a little later in this chapter.

Make Smart Fabric-Buying Choices

Although your sewing machine and tools are a big investment, fabric is what you will spend most of your money on, and as a businessperson, you need to be smart about your purchases.

Although shopping sales and clearance fabrics is a great way to save money, don't let these sales fool you into making poor choices just because the price is less than usual. Make a

plan for what you need, and then if it happens to be on sale, that's a wonderful bonus. Be careful! Don't fall into the trap of buying things you don't need just because the price looks good. Doing a little research and some comparison shopping will help you make better choices. If you want bargains, try eBay, Craigslist, and thrift stores to your heart's content, but be sure that what you buy is what you need and has the quality that you want.

I cannot stress enough how important it is to buy the best-quality fabric that you can. Most customers can spot cheap materials a mile away—don't waste your hard work on something that is not as nice as it could have been if you had only used good-quality fabrics.

Quality Counts

I remember showing my aunt an embroidered tea towel that I had found at an antique market. I was impressed by the delicate stitches and the reasonable price tag. My aunt immediately spotted what my inexperienced eye could not. She said, "The embroidery is lovely, but it's so sad that such beautiful work was wasted on such cheap fabric." When I looked at the fabric, I knew just what she was talking about. It was coarse and thin. I used the towel only a few times before it fell apart and all those delicate stitches were wasted. I imagined those hands working away and wondered why the crafter had used this fabric when for just a little more money the beautiful embroidery would have lasted so much longer and been more valued on good-quality fabric.

Although you may figure out how to get away with using less-expensive fabric and charging more, is that really the relationship you are looking to have with your customers? Remember that they are choosing to buy from you because they want to see a person and a face behind what they purchase. You need to respect this choice by giving them a product that lives up to a high-quality, handmade standard. I would never turn away from a good deal, but it has to be a good deal that still involves good fabric.

Mixing the fabrics in this project was a quick-instinct decision. The bird is made from Amy Butler Lotus Full Moon Polka Dot fabric, the background is from a baby shirt, and the branch came from a vintage brown fabric.

Photo by Virginia Lindsay

Coordinate Fabrics

You can take several routes to make sure your fabrics coordinate effectively. One way is to rely on the designer coordinates. Fabric designers make a whole line to coordinate, and by using only their prints, you can ensure that you have made good choices in your coordinating. I often do this when I am in a hurry and I just want to make something that will look good. This is helpful when sewing for a booth at a show because you know that by using a fabric line you love, your pieces will look great set out in a group. This is also a smart way to begin your sewing-to-sell endeavor because you know that your fabric decisions are getting a helping hand from an accomplished fabric designer.

Another route is to mix fabrics on your own by using your own stash and a few new purchases for inspiration. This has an advantage because you are using your own sense of style, and it will have a special mix based on your unique choices. A typical approach (depending on what you are making) is to choose three fabrics—your showstopper, your second runner-up, and finally your basic supporting fabric. The showstopper is a bold print—maybe a big floral or a large geometric motif. When choosing your runner-up, you usually pick up a color or two from the showstopper print. This fabric has less action going on in the print but still has plenty of interest. It might be polka dots or small flowers. Finally, for the supporting fabric, you have a more uniform color. This is where your small stripes, checkered fabrics, and solids are usually used. The combination of these three will provide you with an interesting and balanced piece.

Eventually, with more experience, you may want to get more creative. After you've gained confidence and experience (or if you are lucky, this may come to you very easily), you can coordinate fabrics by just going with your instincts—no formula needed. Just go with what seems to click together. I have spent a lot of time pulling fabrics off the shelf, looking at combinations, and swapping fabric around, until finally the right ones come together and look great. What a great feeling. This type of coordinating can make your work really stand out, but keep in mind the look of your work as a whole so that things look good together. Getting familiar with the color wheel and basic knowledge of design concepts will help you make good choices. Many good books and websites can help you learn about color and design (see Resources, page 149).

Try Something Different

If it interests you to experiment with different types of fabric and different fabric-altering techniques, your customers will certainly appreciate your effort and creativity. From simple stamping with fabric paint to investing in silk-screening equipment, you can create beautiful and unique fabric almost as easily as you can imagine it. On websites such as spoonflower.com you can design your own fabric and have yardage created (see Resources, page 149).

iPad sleeves by Monica Donohue
of little-pigeon.com

Interview with Monica Donohue of Little Pigeon Crafts

Photo by Monica Donohue

Monica Donohue is a smart and stylish fabric shopper who has created a beautiful line of iPad sleeves and other accessories. Her Etsy shop, Little Pigeon Crafts, is bright and beautiful, and she has been successful by using high-quality fabrics and working hard to develop a wonderful product.

Do you consider yourself a fabric addict? Or are you more pragmatic now that you sew professionally?

When I first began Little Pigeon, I was a self-confessed fabric addict. Often I would purchase fabric on impulse—buying a yard here or 2 yards there. Over the past three years, my business has matured and my approach to purchasing fabric has changed to become more professional.

I still buy fabrics that I love, but I have developed a more methodical approach to introducing new prints into my product offering. I purchase small quantities of the fabric first, and I leave them out in my studio for a week or so to see if I still love them. Then, I try to incorporate it into a mini collection. For example, right now I really love southwestern-themed prints, so I made several items for my shop to see how they will sell. I'm also building my collection of bright, geometric prints.

Once I know I'm still in love with a fabric, I commit to creating a certain number of iPad and MacBook covers from this collection of fabrics, and I purchase enough fabric to reach this goal. After the new items are available for sale, my future fabric purchases are dictated by my customer orders.

This whole method absolutely impacts my buying choices and has curbed my buying impulsivity.

What is your plan when you are shopping for fabric? Do you search sales or hunt for the perfect print and not worry about the price as much?

I have two shopping minds when it comes to buying fabric. My main shopping mind is very price conscious because I am mainly shopping for the supplies I need to replenish the stock of my top-selling products. My secondary shopping mind is less conscious of price. While I browse fabrics for new products in the shop, I don't worry as much about the price.

Although price is a concern, quality is the overriding factor. The fabric quality makes a huge difference in the items I create, and customers appreciate good quality. I decide to buy fabric to create a new design when three important criteria are met: I love the fabric, I am happy with the price, and I can count on the availability of the fabric in the future.

Lastly, I always have a plan when I go fabric shopping. I go to the store or shop online with a list and coupons in hand. Also, I buy in bulk as much as I can, which keeps my prices down.

Do you buy bolts of fabric or just yardage? How do you determine how much to buy? Is it based on the exact number of items you want to sew, or do you just buy based on a feeling of how much you will need?

I buy both bolts and yardage.

In general I try to base how much of a certain fabric I will buy on how many items I have sold over a certain number of months. This allows me to guesstimate how many I may sell in the upcoming months and plan accordingly.

Photo by Monica Donohue

iPad and MacBook covers by Monica Donohue of little-pigeon.com

Do you have a fabric stash of solids and prints so that you can mix each piece individually, or do you plan your iPad covers first and then purchase the fabric?

I do have a big stash of fabrics, but they are mainly the remnants of previous items I have made that I have either discounted or are awaiting an order. In general, I plan my iPad designs first, and then purchase the fabrics. This is based largely on my Etsy shop sales. The process of creating items, photographing them, and listing them online can be quite time-consuming. I have streamlined the process by planning on remaking the item a number of times. Of course, this depends on the demand for the product. Planning my iPad covers also allows me to keep my overhead costs to a minimum so I don't have an overload of scraps.

Do you have any advice for buying fabric on a budget?

I've found it's important to sign up for mailers and newsletters from some of my favorite places to shop, so I know when there is a sale and know when to grab coupons. I never go to the store without a plan or without coupons. For online purchases, I always see if a coupon code is available.

My number-one tip for buying fabric on a budget is to buy wholesale whenever possible. When I first started Little Pigeon, I had two barriers to buying in bulk: First, I didn't know what would sell, and then I was intimidated to apply for wholesale accounts because I thought my order size wouldn't qualify. Over time I've figured out the supplies I always need to have on hand, and I began applying for wholesale accounts. To my surprise, the minimum order may be very low depending on the vendor. Even if your order is for 5 yards or 50 buttons, you may be able to get wholesale pricing—don't hesitate to ask.

What are your favorite places to buy fabric and hardware for your iPad covers?

Some of my favorite places to buy my fabric and hardware are on Etsy, where there are so many amazing sellers and the selection is great. I also really adore Cool Cottons and Bolt Fabric Boutique, both located in Portland, Oregon. There is nothing better than chatting about fabrics with others that love it too.

How do you coordinate fabrics? Do you go by instinct or use a color wheel? Do you have a background in design?

I swoon over beautiful colors, whether they are printed on fabric or painted on canvas. I coordinate fabrics on instinct. If I see a fabric pairing that I like, I will try it out and see what comes of it. Currently I am into neutral fabrics such as beige paired with a color—mint green or tangerine orange are favorites right now. I think neutrals are very appealing to many people and blend well with other bags or clothing people have, while the bit of color makes it come alive. I think simple is better these days. Neutral-toned fabrics for the linings have worked out well for my covers because they go with a lot of prints and are versatile, which streamlines my process for making them.

iPad sleeve in neutral beige and mint green by Monica Donohue of little-pigeon.com

You have a beautiful selection of fabrics. Can you share how you manage to keep it all organized?

My all-time favorite way to store fabric by the cut yard is on hangers. My husband built me a two-tiered closet in my craft studio last year, which was probably one of the best improvements we made to my space. I can easily see what is available, and the fabric stays neat. For fabric that has to be interfaced and cut, I have a shelving system that keeps the pieces flat, organized, and easily accessible. I store completed pieces in large clear plastic totes that are stackable and easy to access in my studio.

SEWING

Like all businesses, your sewing business will change and develop as you become more comfortable with selling. You will be able to see what sells best and what you enjoy making the most—hopefully the two will eventually be the same. The projects in this book are simply a place to begin. Thinking about whom you want to sew for, your own style, and where you want to sell will lead you into a comfortable place where you can be successful.

Change Your Favorite Patterns to Work Better for You

After you have made a pattern several times, you will start to see how you can improve it and put your own stamp on it. Maybe the pockets are too big or too small. Maybe you can use your fabric more efficiently by decreasing the size by a few inches. Make notes while you sew and don't be afraid to make adjustments.

I have a favorite organizer pattern that has three pockets. After sewing it many times for shows, I realized that the third pocket isn't necessary—it adds time onto making the organizer and is not used that much. By eliminating the third pocket, I save time and fabric, without affecting the integrity of the finished product. I also studied the yardage

needed to make it. In the past, I ordered 1 yard of fabric and made three organizers from the fabric with some waste. I did some simple math and realized that if I shortened the length of the pattern by 1″, I could make eight organizers from just 1½ yards of fabric.

Also, consider eliminating or adding details. A little extra time is worth the effort if it makes the project go from ordinary to truly special. A quick addition of a ruffle or some rickrack can take a piece from ordinary to wonderful if done well. Be careful not to get bogged down in fussy details, but a little experimenting can make a big difference. It's also important to realize that good fabric choices can be more effective for sales than detail work.

These lunch bags are popular, and I always sew them for summer shows.

Photos by Virginia Lindsay

Keep Good Notes

When I am sewing for shows or online sales, I often have to look to my pattern instructions to remember how to do a certain step. You would think I would remember because I made the item many times and then took the time to write out detailed instructions. You may have a better memory than I do, but keeping good notes on every item you develop is vital to sewing it easily and efficiently. I once made a really cute wallet for myself, and although I kept the pattern pieces (just slips of unlabeled paper), I have avoided doing that wallet again because I know I will have to start from scratch. Such a waste. Some nice sketches, notes written clearly on paper, and accurate pattern pieces will help to ensure that you don't make mistakes and waste time trying to figure out something all over again.

I sew all these organizers at one time for faster production.

Organize Your Pattern Pieces

One of my biggest problems in the past was keeping my pattern pieces organized so they were easy to find when I needed to sew. When you are learning to sew for a new business, you try so many patterns and ideas that keeping it all organized can become a major nuisance. This is especially true with the popularity of PDF patterns. All those taped-together pieces of paper are hard to wrangle.

First, consider going through all your patterns and being realistic about what you are going to make again. Is that bag you muddled through and then never really used worth keeping? Instead of keeping those iffy pattern pieces, save a copy of the pattern on your computer and recycle the paper. If you really want to make it again, you can print the pattern pieces.

Next, choose your favorites. These are the ones you have made more than once and plan on making again. Carefully fold up all the pattern pieces together and label them. Find a way to store them—plastic bags and file folders work well. Store the patterns in a file cabinet or box. My friend Amy traces all her patterns on kraft paper and writes reminder instructions directly on the paper. On the wall of her sewing room she has a huge corkboard and she thumbtacks her patterns directly onto the board. If you have the space, this is a great way to have all your patterns accessible.

Your patterns are important and vital for sewing efficiently and correctly. You will be using them over and over. Don't let them become torn-up pieces of paper. Consider printing or tracing them onto heavy card stock or poster board. A friend of mine even had her favorite pattern (and best moneymaker) cut from Plexiglas, just like a template you might buy in a store. She uses it repeatedly, without worrying about it becoming damaged. This might not be necessary for you, but making sure you keep all your important patterns and information in good condition, organized, and accessible is worth the effort.

I hang my most-used patterns on a curtain rod with rings and hooks for quick accessibility.

Photo by Virginia Lindsay

Photos by Jessica Fincham

Jessica Fincham of messyjessecrafts.blogspot.com and sewandquilt.co.uk
has a great setup for working.

Organize Your Workspace

When I began sewing, I first used my dining room table and then a tiny
corner of my bedroom for my sewing area. Neither of the spaces was
permanent or functional because I was constantly moving things out of
the way, shoving all my supplies in a box for a quick cleanup, and feeling
generally frustrated with the mess. When we bought our new house, we
had an extra guest bedroom. For about a year, I sewed in that room with
the extra beds and furniture. This was an improvement, but still the space
was for the guests and not for my sewing.

Finally, I realized that although accommodating guests at our house is
important, if I was going to take my sewing seriously, the room needed
to be just for my work. Out went the twin beds (even though they were
brand new and barely slept on), and in came a lot of shelves on the wall, a
cutting table, my ironing board, and a large desk for my sewing machines.
Also, my fabrics and notions came out of the boxes and onto the shelves
so I could see them. Now I had a space to work and be creative.

Store fabric neatly so you can see what
you have.

Commitment to a permanent space to sew is vital to taking your business seriously. You may not have a guest room or a corner of your basement, but you can find something to work for you. Search your home for somewhere you can carve out a place for your sewing machine and materials. It may be only a closet or a corner of a room. Do you really need that closet full of winter coats or can you store those and change that space? Is your cabinet full of unused china really necessary? Sometimes we overlook a space with great potential simply because that room is traditionally used for something else.

After you have your spot, it is time to get planning. Think vertically. Tall bookshelves can hold lots of fabrics and notions without taking up too much space. You can check out an office supply store or a thrift store for a desk that will be a permanent home for your sewing machine—but better yet, get a sewing table that your machine fits into, if available. It might be a splurge, but having the bed of the sewing machine at table height is much more ergonomic. Make your space pretty and fun so that you are inspired to create. You may need to make a small investment, but being organized will be worth it.

Some creative storage solutions include crates, shoe organizers, pegboards for tools, and so on. A friend of mine uses a little cart on wheels for shipping supplies and loves the versatility. Be creative but practical. That cool vintage table may look great, but will it really be useful for your workspace? Professionals make sure their office is attractive *and* practical.

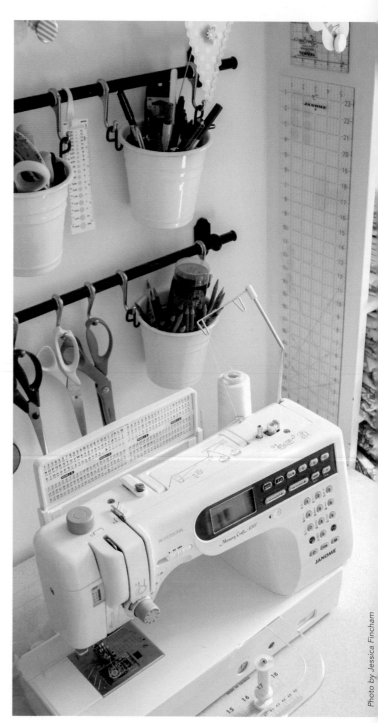

Look for creative ways to organize your workspace.

Photo by Jessica Fincham

SELLING

You can learn about style and fabric all day long, but until you actually decide where you are going to sell, all of this is just talk and no action. Some sewists research and plan their new business until they know so many details about setting up shop that they become experts in the idea of a sewing business but can't quite take the plunge. Others will open shop before you can blink, and although I applaud their adventuresome spirit, *some* planning is needed. Getting your shop started is a process, and it will change and evolve just as you will change and evolve as a businessperson and an artist.

SELECTING A NAME

What's in a name? Pretty much everything, whether you are selling online, at craft shows, or elsewhere. It's how people will find you and all the great things you are selling. Be sure to pick a name that reflects you and products. With the name Virginia, I was given the nickname Ginger by my brother as a child. When I started my company, I wanted a name that reflected me but was also memorable. I made a long list of names off the top of my head, and the name Gingercake was created! It seemed like a fun, memorable name that also reflects my personality. A great fit!

Be sure to pick a name that reflects you and your products.

Below are a few tips:

- Keep the name relatively short and easy to spell—make it easy for your customers to remember the name and find you.

- Keep the name generic enough so that you can expand your offerings if you want. If you choose a name such as JustPurses, you are pretty much stuck with just that.

- What does the name connote? What images does the name suggest when you see it or say it? Think about how the name will help your promote your business.

- Even if you aren't planning on selling online now, you might very well want to in the future. Check around online and make sure no one else is using that name—either in the online marketplaces such as Etsy and Goodsmiths or as a website. If you are thinking of eventually setting up your own website, make sure the URL is available. In fact you might want to buy and register the URL now, so no one else takes it.

Selling Online

A great place to begin selling your goods is online. The advantage of setting up shop and selling online is that you can just make a few pieces and list them in your shop. Your initiation into sales can be slow and steady instead of crazy hours of sewing to make enough for a show. You can sew at your own pace and work as little or as much as you want. Having a few lovely pieces, well photographed and listed in your online shop, is a great place to start. Did you notice the words *well photographed* and *listed*? For many, photographing the work and setting up an online shop sounds like a time-consuming and challenging way to spend an afternoon. Sewists want to sew, not fiddle around with cameras and computers, right?

If you can tolerate the computer time, online selling is ideal for many sewists. You can sew at your own pace and even sew after an order has been placed—if you have sample photos. But honestly, this requires a fair amount of time on the computer when you take this route, beginning with setting up your online shop. Whether you sell on Etsy, Goodsmiths, eBay, or your own website, you will need to create a look that represents your sewing style.

SETTING UP AN ONLINE SHOP

First, take some time to set the style for your shop by designing a banner. Your banner on sites such as Etsy or Goodsmiths will be your shop title. After you go through the initial setup of your shop by giving your name and other basic information, you will be asked to upload a banner. For example, on Etsy, the size of the banner is 760 pixels by 100 pixels. If you are able, you can crop a photo to that size or make fun graphics on your computer to match the correct size. For those of you not confident in your skills with photo cropping and graphics, you can simply buy a banner you like from an Etsy seller. Yes, it can be that easy. And they are so cute and bright and fun.

These shops can make a full set of matching graphics for you, if you like. The only problem is that other shops may use the same style banner and graphics. If that bothers you, you can either learn how to make your own or pay more for a custom banner and optional graphics set. The graphics set will include coordinating reserved listings (items being held for specific customers), custom orders, and even business cards.

Graphics by Jennifer Johnson of studiofortydesign.etsy.com (visit "Business to Business")

TAKING GOOD PHOTOS FOR ONLINE SALES

For more information on how to take photos for online sales, see Projects That Make Best Use of Materials (page 85).

The first step to selling your work online is taking good photos. Although this can be done in many different ways, I am going to share the way I photograph most items for my Etsy shop. A DSLR (digital single-lens reflex) camera is helpful and will give you beautiful photos, but a nice point-and-shoot or even a good iPhone camera can take a nice photo of your sewn items if you are not ready to invest in a DSLR camera and lens.

Lighting

Lighting is the key issue when photographing for your online shop. It is essential that you find the best natural light in your house—bright, indirect, natural sunlight, or find a shady but bright area outside. I bought two white foam core boards from an art supply store as my backdrop for my shop listings. This keeps the background plain and makes the shop items look more uniform because they all have the same backdrop. I also sometimes use an inexpensive reflector to get the light more evenly dispersed.

Using white foam core boards is an easy way to provide uniform backdrops for your items. A reflector is also used to make the subject more evenly lit.

Photo by Virginia Lindsay

If you have a piece that is too big for the foam boards, you can either photograph it against a white wall or some other neutral backdrop—I often use my coat closet door near my front door. I open up my front door and it gives my white closet door lovely natural but indirect light.

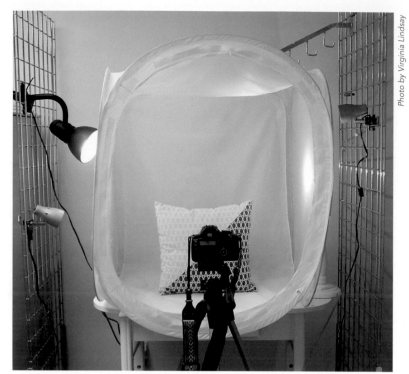

Photo by Virginia Lindsay

A light tent and simple clip-on lamps allow you to shoot small objects with even lighting and a plain background.

Shooting

When you have your piece well lit, take photos of it from several sides and angles.

Consider the special features of your item. Does it have pretty trim detail? Will people want to see the zipper? Are you accurately representing the size? Did you get a shot of the lining or the pocket? Be sure to shoot your piece from several angles for interest, but avoid confusing shots that will make your piece unrecognizable. Try to think of how you would look at something if you were in an actual store and you were considering a purchase yourself.

Photo Editing

After you have taken your photos, upload them to your computer and use a photo-editing program to adjust them so they really look great online. I use iPhoto or Photoshop Elements on my computer, but I have also used Picasa. Other options are GIMP, Photoscape, and Pixlr (for more on photo-editing software, see Resources, page 149). It may take a little time to learn your way around these programs, but after you get the hang of it, you will quickly be able to brighten, crop, and enhance your photos to look beautiful. It is rare, even with a photo from a high-end DSLR camera, to have a photo that can be uploaded onto your computer and be ready for your shop without any editing. In fact, I have never had that happen—even the best photos need a little bit of editing.

If nothing else, try using the built-in option called "enhance photo" (all photo-editing software has this option) to brighten your photo. Make sure you like the result—I often find that it makes the photo too bright and distorts the color, so I usually like to brighten and sharpen my photos myself. If you used the right settings on your camera (read your manual) and used bright, indirect natural sunlight, your editing shouldn't take long.

Try to keep the editing similar in all the photos. Both Goodsmiths and Etsy allow you to upload four photos of each item you list. Make sure to use them all.

Web photos by Virginia Lindsay

Four images of the same item allow you to show all sides on an item for sale.

Tip

When you are posting photos to the Internet, it's important to understand size (usually given in pixels) and resolution (PPI, pixels per inch). A resolution of 72 PPI is usually used. To determine the size for posting, check with the site you are posting to or check community forums for the site. Most photo-editing software programs allow you to resize your photos.

Naming and Saving Photos

When you are done editing, give your photos descriptive names, such as red clutch front, red clutch back, and save them in a special place on your computer so you can find them easily. You will probably want to set up folders and group photos to make them easier to find.

Listing Items

Each online store has specific instructions to list your items. Pay special attention to the titles of your listings. Make it simple and descriptive. People need to be able to search for your item by the title. Something such as "Red Pleated Small Linen Clutch" is much better than "Vintage-Looking Crimson Fancy Wedding Bag Made from European Linen."

Carefully select your categories and tags (again to make it easy for people to find your items) and upload your photos. The last step is to price your item and figure out the shipping costs (refer to Pricing, page 53).

This whole process may take you awhile, and you will fear that you will *never* be able to do this every time you sew something. No worries, though—it gets easier and quicker when you have a system. I usually take photos of several pieces at once, edit them all at once, and create the listings at the same time. To be honest, listing your handmade goods online is not as fun as making them, but after you get the hang of it, you will find yourself able to do the job quickly and efficiently.

One page from my Etsy shop

Selling at Craft Shows

Selling at a craft show is really, really fun. Setting up all your work and talking to the other vendors is a great start to the day. It is fun to meet lots of people and talk up all the wonderful items you have for sale. It's rewarding to see your hard work turn into cash as you pack up at the end of the day with the realization that you are taking home so much less than you brought. That is a great feeling. But honestly, getting ready for a show is hard work. Long hours, repetitive sewing, late nights, and trips to the fabric store at the last minute are all things that will happen if you commit to a craft show. And often that bag you spend waaaayy too much precious sewing time on doesn't sell and you wonder why you didn't just make more tooth fairy pillows instead.

Photo by Virginia Lindsay

Shelves full of handmade items ready for a big show

A very important first step to participating in a show is finding the best show for you to participate in. Investigate the shows in your area and make sure the one you finally join is right for you. Getting ready for a craft show is a lot of work, and not all shows are going to be worth it. You need to research the show in question by looking at websites, calling phone numbers, and contacting vendors. Don't be shy. This is seriously worth your time and effort—if it is hard to find any information about a show, this may be an indicator that the show is not reputable and not well marketed. You may want to plan on attending the show as a consumer to check it out and decide if it's worth participating in the next year.

Popular craft shows often have an application process that has to be completed months in advance. Many times, really big shows are closed to new applicants and are only open to invited artists. This is frustrating, but you should get on the waiting list anyway if you really want to participate in the show in the future.

SETTING UP YOUR BOOTH

Your booth should reflect your style and be a backdrop that best displays your work. Try to think about what you want to display. If your work is bright and colorful, as mine is, you want a fairly neutral backdrop that doesn't compete with what you are trying to sell. I decided to add burlap covers to my white tablecloths to ground my bright fabrics with a more natural fiber. I have also used wooden branches and simple iron baskets. If your work uses more neutral and natural fibers, an all-white booth would be a lovely contrast. Your main goal is to have your booth support your work but not compete with it. If you are a creative person, this can be a fun challenge since creating a booth is an exciting design project.

Photo by Virginia Lindsay

I use burlap to give my bright colors a neutral, natural background.

Plan It Out at Home First

As part of your show planning, find out the size of your booth. Typically you will have at least an 8-×-8-foot space. If you get more experience and want to do bigger outdoor shows, you may want to invest in a tent; those spaces are usually about 15 × 15 feet, which is a luxurious amount of space. A walled tent is a great backdrop to create your own little shop. But as a beginner, you may want to just stick with tables in an indoor facility for your first few shows to see how you like the scene.

Consider making drapes or purchasing yardage to create a wall of fabric that will give your booth the feel of entering a shop and make your customers comfortable. This look can also be achieved with tall accordion-style dividers, bamboo shades, and a garden trellis to make a nice lightweight backdrop. If your event location offers electricity (*and most do not*), plan accordingly with lamps, track lighting, and strands of twinkle lights.

A booth can be arranged in so many different ways, but I have had success by beginning with two tables in an L shape that invites shoppers into the booth. One table is 8 feet long and the other is 6 feet long. These will just fit into the 8-×-8-foot booth. Make sure to find out if the show provides tables; if not, you have to bring your own.

Next, use a table covering that will blend together your tables. I use white sheets and burlap on top. Now you can get creative with fun ways to make your space more vertical. The last thing you want is to have your work piled on a flat table or in baskets on the ground—shoppers won't be able to see everything.

Photo by Virginia Lindsay

Baby Quilts
$65

Fabric Covered Notebooks

Insulated Lunch Boxes

red Pencil Holders

Vertical shelves and baskets provide easily viewed displays.

To create a vertical space I have used an inexpensive garden trellis (painted a fun color), crates and long shelves, modular shoe shelving (but make sure you don't tuck things back in the shoe cubbies because they will easily be overlooked), shutters with hooks, tree branches, and plant stands. Recently I have settled on a white shelving piece I found at a thrift store that is designed to be on top of a dresser. It anchors my booth as a solid piece of furniture but fits nicely on top of a table. I have also acquired a couple of retail iron grids and stands that make hanging up bags and sewn pieces a snap. I also rely on large shallow square baskets and vintage iron baskets. These give each item a separate space and make them more visible to your customer. Many vendors use creative items such as stacked filing cabinet drawers, a clothesline and clothespins, cupcake stands, and old doors. It's fun to get creative.

Do not use rickety old folding tables and heavy pieces of furniture. There is something to be said for using what you have (or in my case, using what my 90-year-old grandmother had in her basement), but it will be embarrassing if your table collapses in the middle of your show. I speak from experience! As for the heavy furniture, unless you have help and know that it will be worth the extra effort, just stick with lightweight things you can carry yourself. You may think that shabby chic dresser is adorable, but it will lose its charm as soon as you have to deal with moving it around, and it is not going to make a big enough difference in your sales.

Photo by Virginia Lindsay

Grids make an easy display.

Photo by Virginia Lindsay

Shema cuffs by Amy Frank of mindfullymadestudios.com displayed on a tiered cake stand

MAKING A PLAN

What will make a difference in your sales is plenty of well-made and useful products. You should start sewing for a show well in advance and make a plan for how much you want to make. If you are not a good planner, you need to really force yourself to change your old habits if you are going to be in a craft show. A professional will give herself plenty of time to sew up enough to make a beautiful display at her show. Below is one idea for a plan that you can modify as needed.

Three Months before the Show

☐ Make a list of what you want to have in your booth. For example, the "To make for show" list (at right) has a mix of small and large items, which will give customers a range of choices and prices. Also, the large duffles and pillows will be great attention getters, and the smaller pieces will work for people who love your work but are on a smaller budget. The list is also only a goal and doesn't have to be met perfectly. Maybe you want to make fewer journal covers and add in some eyeglass holders. Maybe you want to eliminate the wallets and instead add tote bags. This is why you start planning well in advance, so when you make changes, you can adjust easily without having to stay up all night sewing.

To make for show
· 10 pillows
· 15 journal covers
· 10 organizers
· 8 wallets
· 8 messenger bags
· 10 iPad covers
· 10 iPhone covers
· 3 large duffle bags
· 3 small duffle bags
· 8 clutches
· 8 zipper bags
· 10 key fobs
· 3 lap blankets

One Month before the Show

☐ Start planning out your booth and order business cards if you don't already have plenty. Also consider ordering a banner with your company name, or figure out how to make your own. Do you need to shop for display items? Can you raid your family's and friends' basements to find some creative and fun things to use to display goods? Set a budget and stick to it, but budget enough—if you do it on the cheap, your booth will look, well, cheap.

☐ Consider how people will pay you. It's best to have a way to accept credit cards. Fortunately, if you can get cell phone reception or Wi-Fi at the venue, you can use a service such as Square, Intuit, or PayPal and swipe credit cards using a card reader on your smartphone. Don't wait too long to sign up for one of these services; it can take a little while to get your account set up and to receive your card reader. For more information on payment services, see Resources (page 149).

One Week before the Show

☐ Try to stop sewing and work on your booth, pricing, and signage. Who is going to help you set up and break down? If you have to do it alone, make sure you can carry everything yourself. (This happened to me, and it was really hard to move all that stuff alone.) If you are alone, get or borrow a dolly or a wheeled cart. It is best to have a helper if you can find one. Bribe them with handmade items if needed.

Two Days before the Show

☐ Set up your booth at home so you can make sure you have everything you need.

☐ Get cash so you can make change.

One Day before the Show

☐ Pack up everything, including extra supplies such as tape, safety pins, markers, spot cleaner, needle and thread, and so on. Pack up your car and pack up some snacks and drinks for yourself. Get a good night of sleep.

Day of the Show

☐ Get up early and get to the show location to set up everything. Get ready to smile and talk to people all day. No hiding in the back of your booth or keeping your nose in a book. Sometimes I even set up my stool right out in front so I can chat with people who come to my booth or as they walk by.

AFTER THE SHOW

Doing your first show is a lot of work. But after you've done it once, you will know how to set up your booth; you will have your signage, your display props, and probably some merchandise that didn't sell, so it's available for the next show. With a bit more sewing, you'll be ready for your next show. When you get some experience, you can sign up for several shows a few weeks apart, sew a bit more, and then you will see some nice profits.

Consignment Sales

Consignment stores that specialize in handmade goods are nice because you have a store doing the selling and marketing work for you. This may be ideal for someone who wants to just sew and create and not worry about all the computer work and craft show preparation.

You need to find the stores, establish a professional system of keeping track of your inventory, and negotiate the percentage of sales that the store will take. The usual split of a consignment shop is 60 percent for you, the creator, and 40 percent for the store. This means you need to price your goods to make it worth your effort at 60 percent. Also, you will need to keep detailed inventory and check in with your stores often to see if they need more goods. Finding the right store can be a challenge, especially if you live in a small community, but it is certainly worth the effort if you want to diversify.

Promoting Yourself

For more promotion ideas, see Projects That Are Great Sellers (page 113).

As soon as people see your lovely handmade things, they are going to want to remember you. Being able to hand them a little bit of promotional material and directing them to your website is the best way to keep your items in their mind the next time they have a special gift to give. This is where your business cards and website come into play.

BUSINESS CARDS AND POSTCARDS

As a business person, you should have business cards or postcards that include your company name, your name, your website, your email address, and optionally your phone number and address. The cards should represent your style in some way, usually with a photograph or illustration.

Carry your cards with you, so you can hand them out when the conversation turns to what you do. Have your cards available when you sell at craft shows so your customers can pick them up as a reminder. If you are selling online, include a business card or postcard when you mail customers their purchases. If you have customers who don't use the Internet or email, you can mail postcards to them announcing your sales.

USING SOCIAL MEDIA

In our current media-savvy culture, it is crucial for you to be able to use and promote your-self through social media sites. Some of us are better at this than others, but thinking of it as part of your work routine to post updates to your shop, tell people where you are going to be selling, and showing pictures of your current projects is easy and a wonderful way to keep your customers thinking of you.

A good way to be organized about social media is to take advantage of the several media management apps available online. These sites will allow you to schedule a number of posts at once so you keep your audience interested but don't have to spend all your time online (see Resources, page 149).

KEEPING A MAILING LIST

As much as everyone touts the wonderful social media outlets, a good old-fashioned mailing list, and especially an email list, is a great way to reach out to your customers. Send them holiday cards, updates to your shop, your schedule of shows, and general information about your company happenings. I have an email list of every person I have ever sold something to, and I always update them on new styles and promotions that my company is running.

It is important to give your email subscribers an easy way to opt out of your emails, so make sure that the service you use has an easy Unsubscribe link. This will foster a better relationship between you and your customers and help to ensure that no one will complain about your emails (see Resources, page 149).

PRICING AND PACKAGING

Pricing and packaging is often an afterthought when compared with all the loving time and effort you have put into creating your beautiful, handmade items. You may feel as though pricing and packaging are something that has to be finished up quickly and are a nuisance. Nothing could be further from the truth. Pricing is critical to successful selling, and packaging is like the cherry on top of the sundae—you'd feel as though something was missing if it wasn't there.

Ellen Luckett Baker of The Long Thread created this cute card in Photoshop for a craft show as a way to promote her business and keep customers thinking of her long after they have left the craft show. This is a smart idea to make your packaging extra special.

Pricing

It's important to price your work so that you feel good about the price you are asking and your customer feels good about what they are paying. At the very most basic level, a good exchange between two people is when both parties get exactly what they need from the interaction. You need to give your customer value, and your customer needs to compensate you fairly.

In pricing something handmade, look at three things:

- How much did you spend on your materials?

- How much time did it take you to make it?

- How much are people willing to pay for it?

The final question is tricky and it has perplexed creative people for centuries. I cannot give you a formula to answer that final question, but I can help you to figure it out for yourself.

MATERIALS

First, determine your material costs. After you become more accomplished at selling, you will be able to estimate costs quickly in your head. But at first, take the time to break it down. If fabric cost $9.50 a yard and you used ½ yard of fabric for your piece, that's $4.25 to begin. Then you used fusible interfacing at $4.00 a yard and you used ¾ yard, so that is $3.00 more. Then you used a 12″ zipper that was $1.50 and finally some trim that was $0.50. Your total material cost is $9.25. If you shop sales or use coupons, you can get the price of materials down, but the real cost comes next.

TIME

Your time is what really determines the cost. Think clearly about how much you want to make an hour. I remember when I first began my business. After I finished my very first show, I thought about all the time I had spent sewing and realized, in the end, that I made only about $3.50 an hour. If you plan to sell something for $15.00 and it takes you three hours to make and your materials cost $3.00, you need to change something quickly because you'd be making only $4.00 an hour. Realistically, when you begin to sell more, you will see that you almost never make only one thing at a time, so you will have to make some guesstimates. If you want to make $15.00 an hour, you have to plan your projects and work efficiently to make the most of your time in the sewing room. If materials cost you $9.25 and it takes an hour and a half to make your item, a reasonable price to charge would be $32.00, right? Will people pay $32.00 for that item?

Photo by Virginia Lindsay

Bags made by Amy Frank of mindfullymadestudios.com

PRICE

Now back to that third consideration of what people will actually pay. To give you an idea of what people will pay for your handmade item, do some research on Etsy and Goodsmiths first. You will see what other sellers are asking and what they are actually selling. You can say you want to pay yourself $15.00 an hour, but if most buyers pay only $20.00 for similar items, you may not have much success if you are asking $32.00.

This is when you have to make some choices. Charging only $20.00 will bring your hourly wage down to about $7.00 an hour. Ouch. Your skills are worth more than that. But, you may just want to sell some things to get started, and it's okay to start out a little low and learn from your early experiences. If this is unacceptable to you, charge more and see what happens. It's important to evaluate your work also. Is your piece more detailed than the $20.00 pieces? Are you using higher-quality materials? Or, look closely at your piece and maybe you can see where it needs improvement so you can charge more with confidence.

Online it's not as easy to see when you have things priced incorrectly, but pay attention and you will be able to get some clues. If you have many views but no buying, it may be priced too high. Be patient though. If you can wait for the right buyer, you will eventually get your asking price if that many people are looking. If your piece sells right away, and then you list another that sells right away, and then another, then you know that you are not asking enough for your work. The next time you list, charge a little more.

SHOW PRICING

You can use the same basic method for show pricing, but you will need some flexibility and a sense of your customers. If you have your zipper purse priced at $32.00 and person after person picks it up and opens it and shows it to their friends and then walks away, you might want to consider lowering the price. At the same time, if that many people like it, you might be justified in waiting for the customer who is willing to pay the $32.00. This is where you have to make judgment calls for your own business. Only you can decide if you are willing to wait or if you want to sell it more quickly.

Photo by Virginia Lindsay

Packaging

For more ideas on packaging, see Projects That Are Useful Items (page 61).

So you finally make a sale, and now you have to either send the item out in the mail or put it in a bag for your customer at a show. If you are unprepared for this moment, it's not the end of your handmade business to just make do with what you have on hand. But a little preparation for next time will give your business a more professional appearance.

PACKAGING FOR SHOW SALES

Choose a simple and pretty bag to put your item in. I have used clear bags for shows because people are carrying around your item in a bag and others can see it. I have also used kraft-paper bags and I like their simplicity and the options they provide with stamping and using a brand sticker. Choose what you like best for your product. Be sure to include your business card or postcard in the package (see Business Cards and Postcards, page 52).

PACKAGING FOR ONLINE SALES

When packaging your items for mailing, you can take a little more time and effort. People will remember how nice the package from you looked. Along with my postcards, I also have simple stickers made to close up my packages. For mailing, I close up the bag with my sticker and tie a fabric ribbon around it. Sometimes I sew up a kraft-paper bag if the size of the item is something that will work with this type of package. Then, I just slip it into a premade package envelope and mail it off to my customer.

At a show, I put smaller things in kraft-paper bags, but if someone buys one of my pillows, I often put the pillow in a clear bag, fold over the top of the bag, and close it with packing tape. Then I run a fabric strip (often from a vintage sheet since I have a lot of scraps) through the space created by the tape and bag, and the fabric strip becomes a cute handle.

Packaging is a way to get unique and creative, but don't get so caught up in your package that it becomes too expensive and elaborate. Keep it simple and professional, and clearly have your company name showing.

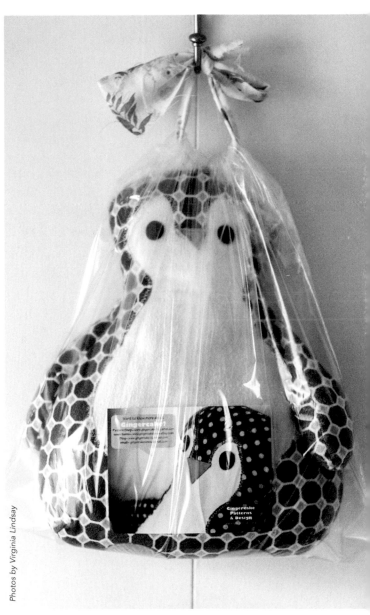

Blessing Band packaging using old pattern tissue by Amy Frank
of mindfullymadestudios.com

Photos by Virginia Lindsay

Interview with Candace Todd of Sparkle Power

Photo by Heather Abbott

Sparkle Power is a shop full of bright and fun handmade items, including tooth fairy pillows, vintage sheet bunting, kids' aprons, and more. Candace has a unique style and has been selling on Etsy since 2007.

I love the fun and colorful items in your online shop, Sparkle Power. Can you tell us about your pricing strategy? Do you have a specific formula, or do you just have a feel for what to charge?

I really just get a feel for an item's price. I start by checking what other sellers may be listing similar items for. Then I consider my cost for materials and the time I put into making the item. I also think about what I would be willing to pay for the product. The price of a product can attract a customer to purchase it, or it can turn them off from purchasing by being either too high or too low. With all of these factors considered, I will ultimately land on a price that I feel comfortable with.

What have you learned about pricing since you opened your shop in 2007? Do you have any examples of mistakes that you learned from or any examples of happy successes?

I have learned that you definitely want to make sure that you are taking care of yourself when it comes to pricing. You need to make sure that you are getting back what you need in order to continue to feel happy working. If you are resenting your work or your customers, you are probably not paying yourself enough and you need to raise your prices.

This chapter covered setting your own hourly earnings and being flexible. How do you make the most of your sewing time so that you are "earning" the wage you set for yourself?

I would love to have an hourly earning schedule set up, but I don't. After my kids are grown, I'll be able to be more structured.

Do you think there are different strategies for pricing at a show versus pricing online? Can you talk about that a little?

I definitely price my products differently at shows than I do online. When people come to shows, there is so much to see and they want to be able to purchase a few different items but still stay within their budget. So I price my items slightly lower for shows. I've found more success this way. Online, people seem to be shopping for specific items, so if your product is photographed and presented well online, it will have no problem selling for the original price.

Packaging is sometimes a hurried event and not much thought is put into it after a sale. What are your thoughts about the importance of packaging?

Putting a little effort into your packaging is very beneficial. A lovely packaged product will make the buyer feel like they are receiving a gift. We all feel happy when we receive gifts. That happy feeling associated with your products may result in them shopping from you again in the future.

Photo by Candace Todd

Napkins by Candace Todd of sparklepower.etsy.com

Packaging ideas from Candace Todd of sparklepower.etsy.com

Photo by Candace Todd

Describe how you package a sale for mailing and how you package a sale at a show.

When I package an item for mailing, I like to include with it a postcard of one of our art prints that they can tack up in their home or use to send a note to somebody. I also include a business card that offers a percentage off their next purchase from my shop. I then wrap the item in tissue paper or a clear bag and seal it with some fun washi tape and baker's twine. I keep it simple but fun.

For shows, you definitely want to package your items well. Think about how you would package them if you were a retail store. Labels and contained packaging can convey a professional feel that is attractive to buyers. Step it up a bit from simply placing your item in a shopping bag for them. At shows you become the owner of your own little physical store space for a short time. So have fun with it and package your items in a way that will attract customers.

Do you have any tips for shopping for packaging or creating your own?

I like to shop at uline.com for basic shipping supplies such as boxes, tubes, or clear bags. I purchase materials such as washi tape, tags, scrapbook paper, and baker's twine when I see them on sale at craft stores or online. You can also get creative with things you may have around the house. Old sewing patterns and book pages are lovely for wrapping items in.

PROJECTS THAT ARE
Useful Items

I love to create sewing projects that are both beautiful and useful. Pillows and decorations are really cute, but nothing is quite as satisfying as making something that will be used almost every day. The following projects are all practical and useful things to sew. They will attract buyers for their beauty *and* because they meet everyday needs.

made to sell

✳ In this section, you'll see the projects as they might be packaged. Take a look at the different possibilities and think about what might work for you. All of the packaging materials are inexpensive and easy to find.

made to sell

SUGGESTED
PRICE POINT

$10 TO **$20**

BOXY PINCUSHION

Finished size: 4˝ wide × 4˝ high × 1½˝ deep

Not only are pincushions fun and satisfying to make, but people also love to buy them for themselves and as gifts. A new pincushion makes your sewing area look fresh again. The shape of this one is practical but pretty too. It holds lots of pins but also fits nicely right next to your machine. Like the Craft Apron (page 66), pincushions will sell to other vendors, DIY shoppers, and those customers dreaming of becoming a seamstress after seeing all your pretty creations.

Supplies

Quilting-weight fabric is recommended. If you are making multiples, plan your materials and cutting based on the number of items you are making to use your fabric efficiently.

- 1 square 6˝ × 6˝ cotton fabric for upper half
- 1 square 6˝ × 6˝ contrasting cotton fabric for lower half
- Polyfill stuffing
- Approximately 1 yard coordinating embroidery floss
- 1 button, 1˝ wide
- Embroidery needle

Stock Your Shelves

To make 7:

- ¼ yard fabric for upper half
- ¼ yard fabric for lower half
- 7 yards floss
- 7 buttons

made to sell

✳ Small items are perfect for cute little boxes. Tie them up with colorful baker's twine—and don't forget your card.

FABRIC: This pincushion features Dear Stella's fabric Do It Yourself Scissors in White and Ann Kelle's Ovals in Lime.

Construction

Seam allowances are ¼″ unless otherwise noted.

1. Pin and sew together the upper and lower pieces, right sides together. Leave a 2″ gap on one side to turn the piece right side out later. **FIGURE A**

2. To make a boxed corner, pinch one corner flat so the seams line up. Pin flat and sew perpendicular to the seams ¾″ away from the tip. Trim away the excess corner fabric, leaving a ¼″ seam allowance. Repeat with the other 3 corners. **FIGURE B**

3. Turn the pincushion right side out and stuff it with polyfill. Use a chopstick to get the polyfill all the way into the corners so it looks nice and full. Hand sew the opening with a blind stitch or ladder stitch.

4. Using the embroidery floss and needle, anchor the thread by making a few backstitches in the center of the bottom of the pincushion. Pull the thread around one side of the pincushion, down through the top at the center, and out the bottom where you first began. Repeat this step to sew around all 4 sides of the pincushion. **FIGURE C**

5. Bring the thread back to the top of the pincushion, and stitch the button in place at the center several times. Knot the floss and clip the end.

Leave open.

A.

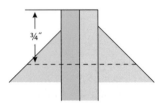

¾″

B.

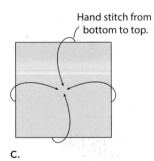

Hand stitch from bottom to top.

C.

Suggestions

Pincushions are so fun to change up and personalize. This is a great opportunity to show some fun style. Mix funky fabric, add hand-sewing details with embroidery floss, and mix up the style of the pincushion top by piecing together various fabrics. The possibilities are endless.

made to sell

CRAFT APRON

Finished size: 17″ × 11″

If you have ever sold items at a craft show, you understand that some of your best customers are other crafters like yourself. When I have a booth, I look forward to the time when I have a chance to walk around and shop the other tables. I love to go to shows where I am not involved at all and can just be a shopper. The craft apron is a great seller not only to other vendors but also to the many DIYers who are shopping. This design is really nice because it has seven pockets to keep you extra organized. Be sure to make one for yourself and wear it all day long at *your* show—you will love how stylish and organized you feel.

Supplies

Quilting-weight fabric is recommended for the pockets and works with a layer of fusible interfacing for the apron body. A heavier-weight fabric would also work for the apron body and eliminate the need for interfacing. If you are making multiples, plan your materials and cutting based on the number of items you are making to use your fabrics efficiently.

COTTON FABRIC

- 2 pieces 12″ × 18″ for apron body
- 1 piece 14″ × 18″ for large pocket
- 1 piece 10″ × 18″ for small pocket
- 2 pieces 3″ × 36″ for ties

OTHER

- 1 piece 12″ × 18″ fusible interfacing if using quilting-weight cotton for apron body
- Air- or water-soluble fabric-marking pen

- *Optional:* Small scrap of lightweight double-sided fusible web

made to sell

✳ For flexible fabric items, roll them up and tie them with a pretty ribbon. Easy!

FABRIC: The apron is made from painter's drop cloth canvas, Kona Cotton in Tangerine from Robert Kaufman Fabrics, and Dolce by Tanya Whelan for FreeSpirit Fabrics.

-------------------------- *Stock Your Shelves* --------------------------

To make 2:

- ¾ yard for apron body
- ½ yard for large pocket
- ⅓ yard for small pocket
- ⅜ yard for ties
- ¾ yard 18″-wide interfacing

To make 4:

- 1⅜ yards for apron body
- ⅞ yard for large pocket
- ⅜ yard for small pocket
- ¾ yard for ties
- 1⅜ yards 18″-wide interfacing

Construction

Seam allowances are ¼″ unless otherwise noted.

PREPARE THE PIECES

1. If you are using quilting-weight cotton for the main piece of the apron, follow the manufacturer's instructions to fuse interfacing to the wrong side of the 12″ × 18″ front apron body.

2. Fold the large pocket in half lengthwise, wrong sides together, to make a folded piece 7″ × 18″. Press the folded edge, pin if needed, and edgestitch along the fold.

3. Repeat Step 2 to fold, press, and stitch the smaller pocket to make a folded piece 5″ × 18″.

4. Test your fabric-marking pen on a scrap of your fabric and make sure the marks will come off easily. Use a ruler to mark the large pocket with a vertical line 6″ in from each end to make 3 even sections. **FIGURE A**

5. On the small pocket, mark a vertical line at the center (9″) and a line 4½″ on either side of the center to divide the pocket into 4 equal parts. **FIGURE B**

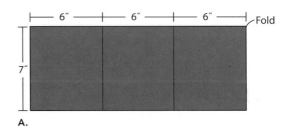

A.

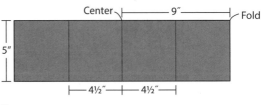

B.

SEW THE DIVIDED POCKETS

1. Layer the small pocket on top of the large pocket, aligning the raw edges at the bottom. Sew through both pockets on the marked center line of the small pocket. **FIGURE C**

2. Layer the pocket unit on top of the front apron body piece, aligning the raw edges at the bottom. Fold (and pin if needed) the small pocket over to the center to expose the 6″ line on the large pocket underneath. Sew on the 6″ line through only the large pocket and the apron body. **FIGURE D**

3. Unfold the small pocket to cover up the line you just sewed. Fold the apron body under toward the center. Sew through just the small and large pockets on the 4½″ line on the small pocket. **FIGURE E**

4. Repeat Steps 2 and 3 to sew the pockets on the other side of the apron.

All this switching up of layers will give you 7 useful and different-sized pockets. **FIGURE F**

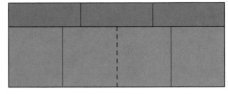

C.

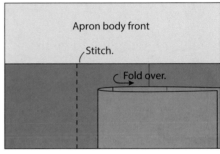

D.

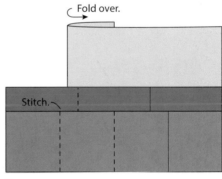

E.

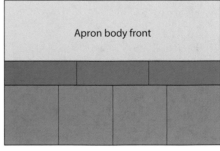

F.

MAKE THE TIES

1. Fold and press the tie strips in half lengthwise, wrong sides together, and then fold and press the raw edges in toward the center fold. Edgestitch both ties closed along the open edges.

2. Pin the ties to the sides of the front apron body ¾″ down from the top edge. Baste in place. Knot the loose ends of the ties together in the center of the apron body and pin them down so they won't work their way back to the edge of the apron body for the next step.
FIGURE G

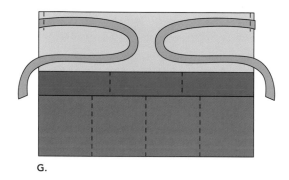

G.

FINISH THE APRON

1. Pin both apron bodies right sides together, starting at the corners. Sew them together with a ½″ seam allowance, leaving a 4″–5″ opening on the top edge.

2. Trim the seams down to ¼″ and clip the corners. Pull the apron right side out through the opening. Poke out the corners with a chopstick, and iron the apron nice and flat. Fold the opening edges in and iron them flat so they match the seam.

3. I like to use a strip of fusible web to close up the opening. This will ensure that the opening looks nice and neat and is practically unnoticeable. Measure the opening and cut a piece of fusible web to fit. Fuse in place according to directions on the package.

If you prefer, blindstitch the opening closed.

4. Finally, edgestitch all the way around the apron to finish it up.

Suggestions

- The ties are long enough so that the apron can either be tied in the back or be crossed in the back and tied in the front.

- If you want to make a quicker version, add just 1 layer of pockets, or have 2 layers of pockets but make them the same size.

- A child's version of this apron would be really cute too. Experiment with the sizing and create a mommy-and-me craft apron set.

made to sell

CLASSIC INSULATED LUNCH BAG

Finished size: 7½˝ wide × 9½˝ high × 5˝ deep (not including tab top)

With four kids, I pack lunches almost every morning. Although I have created many lunch bag styles over the years, this one is a new favorite because it holds a lot of reusable lunch containers, closes easily at the top with hook-and-loop tabs, and has a cute classic look. Lunch bags sell best in the summer and early fall. Stock up on these in June and see them sell like crazy all the way through September.

Supplies

Quilting-weight fabric is recommended. If you are making multiples, plan your materials and cutting based on the number of items you are making to use your fabric efficiently.

- 1 piece 15½˝ × 16˝ main exterior fabric (for front, back, and base)

- 1 piece 10˝ × 18˝ contrasting exterior fabric (for sides and tab top closure)

- 1 piece 8˝ × 10˝ contrasting fabric 2 (*optional* pocket)

- 1½ yards lightweight, nonwoven fusible interfacing, 20˝ wide (I use Pellon 931TD.)*

- 1 piece 10˝ × 32½˝ lining fabric

- 1 piece 10˝ × 32½˝ insulated batting (such as Insul-Fleece by C&T Publishing or Insul-Bright by The Warm Company)

- 7˝ piece of 1˝-wide sew-in hook-and-loop tape

* Interfacing is required only if using quilting-weight cotton. Laminated cotton or sturdy duck cloth would not require interfacing.

✳ Clear bags are great at shows. As your customers walk around, everyone can see what they've purchased.

FABRIC (*for featured project*): Modern Yardage's Cool Jazz, Blumen, and Burst, designed by Liz Ablashi

To make 4:

Follow these cutting instructions. (Do not follow the diagrams for the rest of the project.)

- ⅔ yard main exterior fabric

  Cut 2 strips 8″ × WOF*; subcut into 10″ pieces.
  Cut 1 strip 5½″ × WOF; subcut into 8″ pieces.

- ⅝ yard contrasting exterior fabric

  Cut 2 strips 5½″ × WOF; subcut into 10″ pieces.
  Cut 2 strips 3½″ × WOF; subcut into 8″ pieces.

- ⅓ yard contrasting fabric 2

- 4½ yards 20″-wide interfacing

  Cut 8 strips 8″ wide across the interfacing; subcut into 10″ pieces.

  Cut 12 strips 5½″ wide across the interfacing; subcut into 16 pieces 10″ wide and 8 pieces 8″ wide.

  Cut 8 strips 3½″ wide across the interfacing; subcut into 8″ pieces.

- 1 yard lining

  Cut 2 strips 8″ × WOF; subcut into 10″ pieces.

  Cut 3 strips 5½″ × WOF; subcut into 8 pieces 10″ wide and 4 pieces 8″ wide.

- 1 yard insulated batting

  Cut 2 strips 8″ × WOF; subcut into 10″ pieces.

  Cut 3 strips 5½″ × WOF; subcut into 8 pieces 10″ wide and 4 pieces 8″ wide)

- 28″ hook-and-loop tape

* WOF = width of fabric

Construction

Seam allowances are ¼″ unless otherwise noted. Backstitch or lockstitch at the beginning and end of all seams.

PREPARE THE PIECES

1. Cut the fabric according to the list and the three cutting diagrams (below and next page).

Main exterior fabric: 2 rectangles 8″ × 10″ and 1 rectangle 5½″ × 8″

Contrasting exterior fabric: 2 rectangles 5½″ × 10″ and 2 rectangles 3½″ × 8″

Lining: 2 rectangles 8″ × 10″, 2 rectangles 5½″ × 10″, and 1 rectangle 5½″ × 8″

Interfacing: 4 rectangles 8″ × 10″, 4 rectangles 5½″ × 10″, 2 rectangles 5½″ × 8″, and 4 rectangles 3½″ × 8″

Batting:
2 rectangles 8″ × 10″,
2 rectangles 5½″ × 10″,
and 1 rectangle 5½″ × 8″

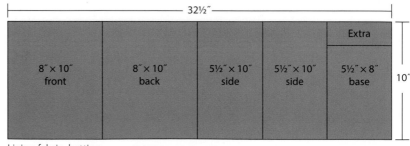

Lining fabric, batting

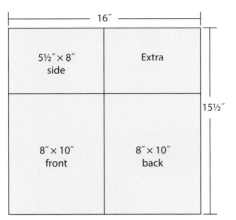

Main exterior fabric

16″	
5½″ × 8″ side	Extra
8″ × 10″ front	8″ × 10″ back

15½″

Contrast exterior fabric

18″			
		Extra	
5½″ × 10″ side	5½″ × 10″ side	3½″ × 8″ tab	3½″ × 8″ tab

10″

Tip

You can fuse larger pieces of interfacing to the back of your fabrics before cutting, and then cut the fabric and interfacing all together. What you waste in materials, you may save in time.

2. Fuse the corresponding interfacing pieces to the back of all the quilting-weight cotton pieces.

3. Baste the batting pieces to the wrong side of the corresponding exterior pieces, using a ⅛″ seam allowance. (You can also skip the basting and just pin the exterior and batting pieces together as you go).

4. *Optional:* Fold the 8″ × 10″ pocket piece in half, wrong sides together, so that the folded piece is 5″ × 8″. Press and topstitch along the folded edge.

5. Fold the 3½″ × 8″ rectangles for the tab closure in half lengthwise, wrong sides together, so that the folded piece is 1¾″ × 8″. Finger-press to crease, and unfold. Pin 1 piece

of hook-and-loop tape to the right side of the tab, centered and ¼″ away from the fold. Sew around all 4 edges of the tape. Sew the other piece of the tape to the remaining tab the same way.

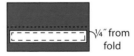

¼″ from fold

6. Refold the tabs on the center crease, right sides together. Pin and sew the short edges. Clip the corners and turn right side out. Press flat on the side *without the hook-and-loop tape.*

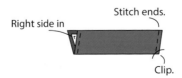

Right side in
Stitch ends.
Clip.

CONSTRUCT THE LUNCH BAG BODY

1. Using a straightedge and a pencil (or some light marking tool), mark a line on the wrong side of the 5½″ × 8″ lining base piece ¼″ in from each side. Repeat with the 5½″ × 8″ batting base piece. These lines will make it simple and accurate to sew the sides later.

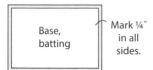

Base, batting

Mark ¼″ in all sides.

2. Pin the 5½″ × 8″ exterior base piece to a 5½″ × 10″ exterior side piece, wrong sides together (in this case, batting sides together), along the short sides. Sew with the base facing up, starting and stopping your stitching line ¼″ in from the corners, using the lines drawn in Step 1.

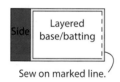

Side

Layered base/batting

Sew on marked line.

3. Repeat Step 2 to attach the other 5½″ × 10″ exterior side piece to the base.

4. *Optional:* Layer the pocket on top of the 8″ × 10″ exterior front piece, aligning the raw edges at the bottom and sides. Pin or baste in place.

5. Repeat Step 3 again to attach the exterior front and back pieces to the base.

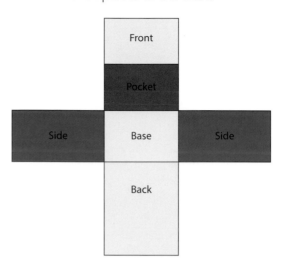

Front

Pocket

Side | Base | Side

Back

6. Fold the exterior bag from a corner of the base so the front and an adjacent side meet. Pin them right sides together and sew from the top down, again stopping ¼″ short, just like with the base. Repeat this step to sew up all the side seams.

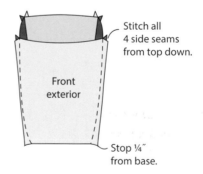

Front exterior

Stitch all 4 side seams from top down.

Stop ¼″ from base.

7. Trim the seams and clip the corners. Turn the exterior bag right side out and press.

8. Repeat Steps 2–6 with the lining pieces, but make sure to *leave a 4″ gap in one of the lining sides* so you can turn the entire piece right side out later. Clip the corners of the lining.

ATTACH THE HANDLES AND FINISH THE BAG

1. Pin the tabs to the top of the bag exterior, at the front and back, right sides together, with the hook-and-loop side of the tabs away from the bag. Baste in place with an ⅛″ seam allowance.

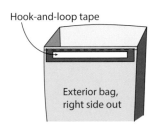

Hook-and-loop tape

Exterior bag, right side out

2. Insert the exterior bag inside the lining, right sides together, and line up the seams at the top. Pin and sew around the entire opening.

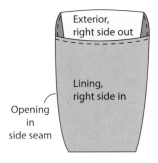

Exterior, right side out

Lining, right side in

Opening in side seam

3. Trim the seam around the top edge and then reach inside the opening left in the lining. Pull the exterior bag out and then pull the lining right side out too. Push the lining inside the exterior body.

4. Pull the lining back out and press the raw edges of the lining opening under. Either blindstitch the opening closed or topstitch it closed as close to the edge as possible. Push the lining back inside the bag.

5. Press the bag well, paying special attention to the opening.

6. Topstitch around the bag opening. Close the bag at the hook-and-loop tabs; push in the sides to make the classic lunch bag look. Iron the sides in or just fold the bag neatly and let the fabric "train" itself to naturally close with the sides in.

Suggestions

- You can make additions to this bag, including a zippered pocket, pockets on both sides, or interior pockets.

- You can also really simplify the bag for a quick sew by having no pockets, using all one fabric, eliminating the Insul-Fleece batting, or changing the closure to a button and elastic cord. So quick and easy.

- Try appliqué, patchwork, or trim to dress up the lunch bag and show your sewing strengths.

made to sell

SUGGESTED
PRICE POINT
$35 TO **$50**
*(SET OF 4 PLACE MATS AND
4 NAPKINS)*

YOUR BEST PLACE MAT AND NAPKIN SET

Finished size: 12″ × 18″ place mat, 17″ × 17″ napkin

Anyone can make a superquick place mat by sewing two layers of fabric together, but a beautiful, sturdy, reversible, bound place mat? This will be valued by your customers. Add coordinating cloth napkins for a truly lovely set. Use high-quality, stylish fabrics and this makes a perfect handmade gift.

Supplies

Quilting-weight fabric is recommended. If you are making multiples, plan your materials and cutting based on the number of items you are making to use your fabric efficiently.

For 4 place mats and napkins:

- ⅔ yard each or 1 piece 24″ × 36″ each of 2 different cotton fabrics for place mat top and backing

- ⅓–⅔ yard or 1 piece 24″ × 36″ cotton batting, depending on the width of your batting

- 3 yards lightweight fusible interfacing, 20″ wide

- ½ yard coordinating fabric for straight-grain binding or packaged double-fold binding to equal 7 yards

- 1 yard or 1 piece 36″ × 36″ cotton fabric for napkins

made to sell

✳ Package items together that will be used together. A simple tie and a blank card allows space for a personal note.

FABRIC: I used a mix of Dear Stella's Piper fabric line.

Place Mat Construction

Seam allowances are ¼″ unless otherwise noted.

PREPARE THE PIECES

1. Cut the batting and the 2 fabrics for the place mats into 4 pieces 12″ × 18″ each (12 pieces total). Cut the interfacing into 8 pieces 12″ × 18″. Be accurate and careful in your cutting for best results. A rotary cutter, rotary cutting ruler, and cutting mat are invaluable here.

2. Following the manufacturer's instructions, fuse interfacing to the wrong side of the 8 fabric pieces.

3. Sandwich a batting piece between 2 different place mat pieces, both right sides out. Pin together at the corners. Serge or zigzag around the outer edge of all 3 layers if desired. Otherwise, the pins will hold it together fine, or you can baste the layers together if desired. Repeat to make 4 place mats.

MAKE AND SEW THE BINDING

1. If you are making your own binding: Cut 7 strips 2¼″ × WOF* from the binding fabric. Sew the short ends together and press the seams open to make 1 continuous strip. Fold and press the binding strip, *wrong* sides together.

2. Use the continuous binding strip (or purchased binding) to bind each place mat using your favorite (and fastest) method. For more on binding, see Two at a Time Oven Mitt, Steps 7 and 8 (page 84).

* WOF = width of fabric

Napkin Construction

1. Cut the napkin fabric into 4 pieces each 18″ × 18″. Taking the time to make nice square cuts makes a big difference here.

2. With the 18″ × 18″ napkin fabric square wrong side up, draw a diagonal line 1″ in from the tip at each corner. Repeat to mark all 4 napkins. **FIGURE A**

3. Fold fabric right sides together through the corner, aligning the raw edges, so the drawn line makes a right triangle. Measure or estimate the center of the visible line and pin to mark. Repeat this step to pin all 4 corners on all 4 napkins. **FIGURE B**

4. Using the drawn line as your guide and starting at the folded edge, sew along the line to the pin, about ½″. Sew all 4 corners on all 4 napkins. You may want to chainstitch the corners without cutting threads to save time. **FIGURE C**

5. Clip off the tips of the corners and make a tiny clip in the remaining seam allowance at the fold. Gently push all the corners out to the right side with a chopstick. **FIGURE D**

6. Iron the napkin, right side down, so the edges are flat, as guided by the corner seams. Then fold and iron the raw edges under to meet the crease. The space left when you sewed only half the corner will guide you to make a nice mitered corner. **FIGURE E**

7. When you have ironed all 4 sides under, don't bother to pin. Just take the napkin over to your sewing machine and sew the folded edge down around the 4 sides of the napkin.

8. Repeat with the 3 other 18″ × 18″ pieces of fabric. Iron nice and flat.

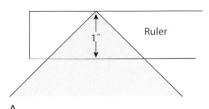

A.

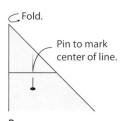

B.

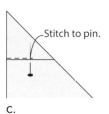

C.

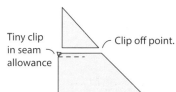

D.

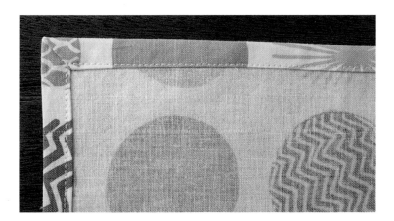

Suggestions

- Use thicker but still washable fabric instead of the quilting-weight fabric so that you can eliminate the fusible interfacing step. For example, cotton twill or a lightweight canvas would work well.

- Patchwork on place mats is always a big hit, but watch out for how time-consuming it can become. Remember that place mats have to be in a certain price range in order to sell easily.

- Quilt your place mats before binding for extra durability.

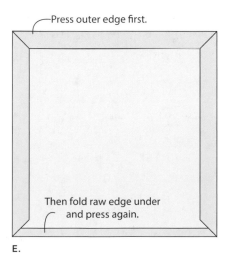

E.

made to sell

TWO AT A TIME OVEN MITT

SUGGESTED
PRICE POINT
$25 TO **$32**
PER PAIR

Finished size: 8½″ × 10″ each

A person can never have enough potholders and oven mitts, especially beautiful, handmade ones. This oven mitt is great because you make two at once. A set of oven mitts is always better than one! Enjoy mixing up fun fabric combinations and make a truly useful and pretty kitchen accessory.

Supplies

Quilting-weight fabric is recommended. If you are making multiples, plan your materials and cutting based on the number of items you are making to use your fabric efficiently. You need a ¼-yard cut of each material and will have a little left over.

- 1 piece 9″ × 35″ fabric for the lining

- 1 piece 9″ × 35″ fabric for the exterior

- 1 piece 9″ × 35″ cotton batting (I use Warm & Natural.)

- 1 piece 9″ × 35″ insulated batting (such as Insul-Fleece by C&T Publishing or Insul-Bright by The Warm Company)

- At least 80″ of ½″-wide double-fold bias tape (I suggest making your own bias tape because the stretch is better. You need about ½ yard of fabric, or a 17″ × 17″ square, to make enough bias tape.)

✳ Add a creative touch to a plain brown shipping bag. A simple zigzag stitch here makes it unique.

FABRIC: I used Michael Miller Fabric's Technicolor by Emily Herrick and coordinating Cotton Couture solids.

Construction

Seam allowances are ¼˝ unless otherwise noted.

1. Layer your exterior fabric right side down, then insulated batting, then cotton batting, and finally the lining fabric right side up. Baste the layers together as needed.

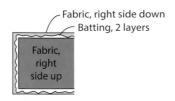

Fabric, right side down
Batting, 2 layers
Fabric, right side up

2. Quilt the layers using your favorite method. I like to do gently swerving lines running the length of my quilt sandwich since it is fast and looks nice, but if quilting is one of your strengths, this is a chance for you to show your skills.

3. Cut the long piece into 4 pieces: 2 pieces 8½˝ × 10˝ for the back and 2 pieces 8½˝ × 7˝ for the front.

```
├─ 10˝ ─┼─ 10˝ ─┼─ 7˝ ─┼─ 7˝ ─┤
┬  8½˝ × 10˝ │ 8½˝ × 10˝ │ 8½˝ × 7˝ │ 8½˝ × 7˝
9˝     back  │   back    │  front   │  front
┴
```

4. Use your favorite (and fastest) method to bind one 8½˝ end of your 8½˝ × 7˝ pieces. If your fabric has a directional print, bind the upper edges.

5. Layer a smaller bound piece on top of each of the 8½˝ × 10˝ pieces, lining sides together, aligning the raw edges at the bottom and sides. Pin together in the center.

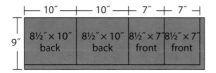

├─ 8½˝ ─┤
Bind 8½˝ edge.
10˝
7˝

6. Copy or trace the Oven Mitt pattern (pullout page P2) and cut it out. Use the pattern to cut the curved corners through both of the layered pieces at the same time.

Trim through both pieces.

Tip

Special binding feet are available to guide the prefolded binding around the edge for perfect stitching, which can speed up this technique.

7. Baste the 2 trimmed pieces together ⅛˝ from the raw edges. If you prefer, baste by machine on the longest stitch setting, but hand basting works a little better for me.

Baste pocket to back.

8. *Optional:* If you're an experienced sewist and great at machine binding, use my fast way to finish the binding ends in advance: Cut 2 pieces of bias binding 28˝ long (the perimeter of the oven mitt plus ½˝ for seam allowances). Open them up and sew the short ends, right sides together, to make 2 loops. Finger-press the seam out and press the binding back into its original shape.

9. Bind the 2 mitts using your favorite binding method. Stop sewing close to where you started stitching, trim the excess, fold the raw edge under, and keep sewing back to where you started.

Suggestions

• Hand binding gives a beautiful finish, but make sure to add this extra time into your final asking price. People are willing to pay only so much for potholders, so figure out whether hand binding is worth it.

• Showcase your skills by combining prints to make beautiful and colorful oven mitts.

• Forget the quilting and just layer, cut, and bind for superfast mitts that are still really nice.

PROJECTS THAT MAKE
Best Use of Materials

Although I love making scrappy fabric projects with my extra fabric bits, what I love even more is sewing something that uses fabric so efficiently that I don't have enough leftover fabric to add to my scrap bin. The projects in this chapter fit this category and will be great sellers in your shop.

Because of the efficient nature of these project instructions, the fabric requirements don't include extra yardage to cover mistakes or to round up to quantities sold in fabric shops, so take that into consideration when choosing fabrics.

made to sell

* For this section, you'll see the projects as they might be photographed for online sales. In addition to seeing the final photos, you'll see the photo setup. Keep in mind that you may need to take different photos for different sites—look around the sites you plan to sell on and see the type, size, and number of photos that the sellers use.

made to sell

**SUGGESTED
PRICE POINT**

$15 TO **$25**

DRAWSTRING BACKPACK

Finished size: 13½˝ × 16½˝

When I saw these becoming popular a few years ago, I kept thinking,
"I can make that." Well, it's true … anyone who can sew can make
this bag easily. What's fun about the style of this little backpack is
that it is full of potential for all sorts of bright prints and fun uses.
You can make ten of these quickly using beautiful fabrics, and your
customers will love how useful and cute they are.

Supplies

*Quilting-weight fabric is recommended. If you
are making multiples, plan your materials and
cutting based on the number of items you are
making to use your fabric efficiently.*

- 1 piece at least 14˝ × 36˝ cotton fabric for
  exterior

- 1 piece at least 14˝ × 36˝ cotton fabric for lining

- 8˝ of rickrack or ½˝-wide ribbon

- 4 yards of ⅛˝-diameter nylon cording

made to sell

* Lighting setup: Natural light from the window; a white foam core board
  (on the right, not seen) bounces light to fill shadows; a black foam core
  board blocks unwanted reflection from the floor.

FABRIC: I used some bright and fun fabric from the Moxie line by Erin McMorris
for FreeSpirit Fabrics to go with the youthful feel of this project.

Construction

Seam allowances are ¼˝ unless otherwise noted. Backstitch at the beginning and end of each seam.

MAKE THE EXTERIOR AND LINING

1. Cut both the exterior and lining fabrics into 2 pieces each (4 total) 14˝ × 18˝.

2. Cut the rickrack into 2 pieces 4˝ long. Fold the rickrack piece in half to make loops. Aligning the raw edges, pin each loop in place 1˝ up from the bottom of 1 exterior bag piece, right side up, as shown. **FIGURE A**

3. Pin both exterior bag pieces, right sides together, with the loops sandwiched in between. Mark 2˝ down from the top in the seam allowance on the wrong side of 1 bag piece. Starting at the mark, sew down one long 18˝ side, pivot and stitch across the bottom, and pivot and stitch up the other long side, stopping at the other mark 2˝ from the top edge. **FIGURE B**

4. Clip the corners. Clip **to**, *but not through*, the side seam allowances where seams begin and end. Turn the bag exterior right side out. Press.

5. Repeat Steps 3 and 4 with the lining pieces, but make sure to *leave a 4˝ gap* at the bottom of the lining so you can turn the bag right side out later. Do *not* clip the seam allowances. **FIGURE C**

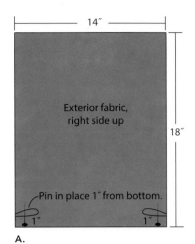

A.

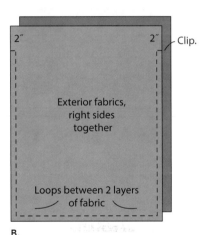

B.

Leave open.

C.

---- *Stock Your Shelves* ------------------

To make 3:

- 1 yard each of exterior and lining fabric (requires 42˝ usable width of fabric)

- ⅔ yard trim

- 12 yards cording

6. Insert the bag exterior into the bag lining, right sides together, and line up the upper raw edges and the side seams.

7. On one side of the bag *only*, pin the lining and exterior pieces together along the upper edge of the bag and down the open 2″ where the side seam stopped. Flip the exterior seam allowances out at the clip to meet the raw edges of the lining.

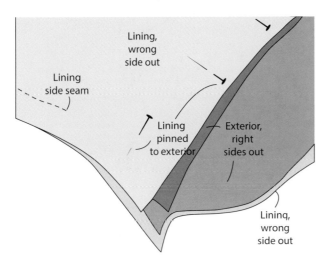

Lining, wrong side out

Lining side seam

Lining pinned to exterior

Exterior, right sides out

Lining, wrong side out

8. Starting where the side seam stopped, and making sure to backstitch or lock your stitches, continue sewing up the open side (this time through 1 lining and 1 exterior piece instead of both exterior pieces or both lining pieces). Pivot at the corner, stitch across the upper edge, pivot at the opposite corner, and stitch down the side, stopping and backstitching at the opposite side seam.

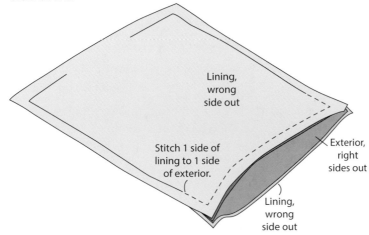

Lining, wrong side out

Stitch 1 side of lining to 1 side of exterior.

Exterior, right sides out

Lining, wrong side out

9. Repeat Steps 7 and 8 on the opposite side of the bag with the remaining open lining and exterior edges.

10. Turn the bag right side out through the opening in the lining. Push the lining inside the exterior. Reach through the opening in the lining and poke out the exterior corners with a chopstick. Pull the lining back out and press the raw edges of the opening inside. Sew the opening closed, either by hand with a blind stitch or by machine with an edge stitch, as close to the edge as possible. Push the lining back inside the bag a final time and press the upper edge of the bag nice and flat.

MAKE THE CASING

1. Fold the upper edge of the bag down 1″ to the outside and press flat. Pin all around the bag and sew the folded edge down about ⅛″ from the seam. If your machine has a free arm, use it to make it easier to sew all around.

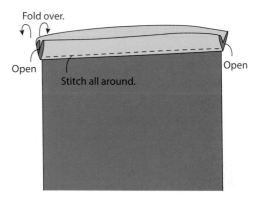

2. Cut the cording into 2 equal lengths.

3. Use a safety pin or bodkin at one end of a piece of cord to thread it through one side of the casing. When you get to the opening on the other side, continue through the other side until you are back where you began. Take off the safety pin and gently pull the cord through the casing (without drawing up the casing) so that both ends are even. Thread one of the ends through the loop at the bottom of the bag and then tie the ends together in a tight knot. Apply Fray Check to the cut ends, if you like. **FIGURE D**

4. Repeat Step 3 with the other piece of cord, starting at the opposite end of the casing. **FIGURES D & E**

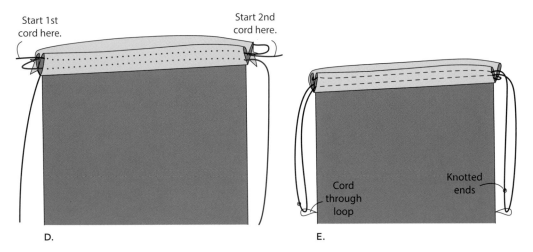

5. *Optional:* To add a little more structure to the bag, poke out the bottom corners of the bag, line up the bottom and side seams, and flatten the corner into a triangle shape. Pin flat and mark a line with chalk or removable ink 1½˝ from the tip of the corner. Sew on the line, making sure not to catch the loop or drawstring.

6. Pull the drawstring cords from opposite ends and gather the casing to make a stylish and functional backpack that your customers will love.

Suggestions

• Adding a pocket would be a fun and easy addition to the front or sides of the backpack.

• Experiment with different types of fabric and patchwork, but don't get too bulky because the drawstring won't work as easily with thick fabrics.

made to sell

SUGGESTED
PRICE POINT
$14 TO **$18**

QUICK AND COOL GROCERY TOTE

Finished size: 17″ × 21″

This quick and clever grocery tote will help your customers look stylish on their trips to the store. The tote requires two ½-yard cuts of fabric (1 yard total) and leaves little waste. After you get the hang of it, you can sew a bunch at once. Selling them in sets with matching fabrics would be adorable.

Supplies

Quilting weight fabric is recommended. If you are making multiples, plan your materials and cutting based on the number of items you are making to use your fabric efficiently.

- ½ yard cotton fabric for exterior*

- ½ yard cotton fabric for interior*

- Coordinating thread

* Choose fabric with a 44″ usable width. If your fabric is just a bit narrower, after prewashing and trimming selvages, your bags will be just a little bit shorter.

made to sell

made to sell

✳ Lighting setup: An interesting hanging hook; natural light from the window hits the bag at a 45° angle; a white foam core board (on the right), about 8″ away, bounces light to soften shadows.

FABRIC: I used some fun Michael Miller basics for these grocery totes in Lime and Tangerine.

Construction

Seam allowances are ¼″ unless otherwise noted.

PREPARE THE PIECES

Make sure both of your fabrics are the same width (standard widths can vary from company to company). If not, trim the wider one to match the narrower fabric.

1. Fold each piece of fabric in half, selvage to selvage, so that it is 18″ × 22″.

Then fold each in half again in the opposite direction to 9″ × 22″. Trace and cut out the Grocery Tote pattern (pullout page P1). Place the pattern on the folded fabric, following the placement instructions on the pattern. The pattern should fill up your whole folded piece. If the pattern piece is too big, simply fold the pattern at the bottom to fit your folded fabric.

2. Cut 1 bag pattern piece from each fabric.

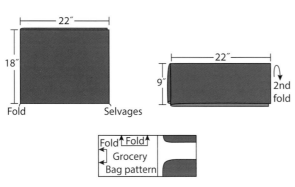

MAKE THE BAG

1. Unfold the cut pieces. Refold the exterior piece, right sides together, along the fold at the bottom. Pin and sew the side seams.

Repeat this step with the lining, making sure to leave a 4″ opening on a side seam for turning.

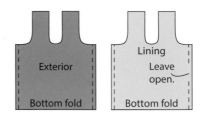

2. Put the bag lining inside the exterior bag, right sides together. Match up the side seams. Pin and sew together all 4 curves between the straps. Leave the ends of the straps open. Clip the curves.

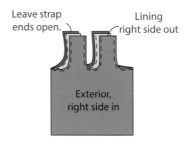

MAKE THE CORNERS

1. Pull the interior and exterior apart (but leave them wrong sides out for now) and lay the piece flat. Mark the corners 1, 2, 3, and 4 as shown.

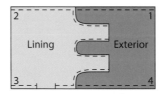

2. Pull apart all 4 bottom corners so the side seam is now in the center of each corner, making a triangle shape.

3. Layer corners 1 and 2 together, aligning the side seams. Pin together; then mark a line 3½″ from the tip of the corner on top.

4. Making sure the corner is flat and smooth, stitch on the drawn line through both the lining and the exterior.

5. Repeat Steps 3 and 4 to sew together corners 3 and 4.

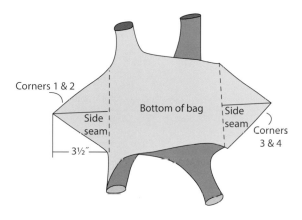

6. Trim off both corners ¼″ from the seam.

FINISH THE BAG

1. Reach into the opening on the side of the lining and pull the piece right side out. Then push the exterior bag inside the interior. Use a pencil or chopstick if needed to push out the handles.

2. Pull the lining back out and press the seam allowances under to the wrong side. Close the opening either with a blind stitch by hand or a top stitch by machine as close to the edge as possible.

3. Push the lining back into the bag and press the entire bag nice and flat, making sure all seams are fully extended.

4. *On one side of the bag only*, fold and press the open, raw edges of 2 handles ½″ to the wrong side.

5. Insert the open ends of the opposite 2 handles inside the folded handle ends. Pin closed and topstitch through all layers close to the fold to connect the handles. *Optional:* At this point the bag can be finished if you like the shape of nice, wide handles.

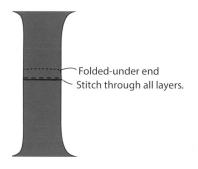

Folded-under end
Stitch through all layers.

6. At the handle seams, fold the sides in to meet at the center. Pin and sew across the folded handle on the seam.

Suggestions

• Make sets of these bags and market as a cute gift pack.

• Choose bright and fun fabrics to make your customers happy about using reusable bags.

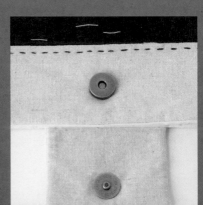

made to sell

TABLET SLEEVE

Finished size: 8¼″ × 10″ (as photographed)*

People love their electronic gadgets, and covering them with a beautiful handmade sleeve is a great way to soften up their hard lines. This project gives you the measurements to make an iPad cover or an iPad Mini cover (which will also fit a Kindle Fire and a Nook). At a show, I suggest bringing two sizes and offering to take special orders.

Supplies

Quilting-weight fabric is recommended. If you are making multiples, plan your materials and cutting based on the number of items you are making to use your fabric efficiently. Measurements are for an iPad 2/3/4 cover (the largest size) with variations for other, smaller tablets at the end of the project.

made to sell

- 1 piece at least 9″ × 9″ cotton fabric for exterior top and tab

- 1 piece at least 9″ × 17″ cotton fabric for exterior body

- ¾″ round magnetic snap

- ½ yard fusible interfacing, 20″ wide (I use Pellon 931TD.)

- 1 piece at least 9″ × 22″ lining fabric

- 1 piece at least 9″ × 22″ batting (I use Warm & Natural.)

made to sell

> * Lighting setup: Natural light from a window (on the left); white foam core boards create a lightbox, bouncing light for soft shadows and even light.

FABRIC: For this project sleeve, I used Michael Miller's Waterfront Park/Bridgetown fabric in Navy by Violet Craft.

* For other size options, see Size Variations (page 98).

Construction

Seam allowances are ⅜″ unless otherwise noted.

PREPARE THE PIECES

1. Cut the fabrics to the following sizes:

- Cut the 9″ × 9″ piece into 2 pieces 9″ × 3″ for the exterior top and 2 pieces 4″ × 3″ for the tab. Cut the 9″ × 17″ piece into 2 pieces 9″ × 8¼″ for the exterior body.

- Cut the lining and batting each into 2 pieces 9″ × 10¾″.

- Cut the interfacing into 2 pieces 9″ × 10¾″ and 2 pieces 4″ × 3″.

2. Follow the manufacturer's instructions to fuse interfacing to the wrong side of the 2 tab pieces.

MAKE THE SLEEVE

1. Pin and sew the 2 lining pieces, right sides together, pivoting at the corners and leaving a 4″ gap across the bottom for turning. **FIGURE A**

2. Pin and sew the 9″ × 3″ exterior top and 9″ × 8¼″ exterior body pieces, right sides together, along the long edges, using a ¼″ seam allowance. Press the seam allowance open. Repeat with the other exterior pieces.

3. Fuse interfacing to the wrong side of both assembled exterior pieces. Pin batting to the wrong side of each exterior piece. Topstitch on either side of the seam on both exterior pieces. **FIGURE B**

4. Pin and sew the 2 exterior pieces, right sides together, pivoting at the corners. Trim the corners. Turn the exterior right side out, poke out the corners, and press flat.

Leave open.

A.

Make 2.

B.

Size Variations

For the iPad Air (6¾″ × 9½″), you can adjust this pattern by subtracting 1½″ from all the body cut widths.

The iPad Mini, Kindle Fire, and Nook are all about 5½″ × 7½″. Simply subtract 2″ from both the height and width of the body pieces and cut the tab as directed:

- Cut the lining pieces 7″ × 9″.

- Cut the exterior pieces 7″ × 2½″ (upper) and 7″ × 6¾″ (body).

- Cut the tab pieces 2½″ × 3½″.

MAKE THE TAB

1. Pin the 2 fused tab pieces right sides together. Sew around both short sides and one long side, pivoting at the corners. Trim the corners. Turn the tab right side out, push out the corners, and press. **FIGURE C**

2. Follow the manufacturer's directions to install the male half of the magnetic snap on the underside of the tab, ½″ in and centered along the long sewn edge. **FIGURE D**

ASSEMBLY

1. Center the tab as shown on the upper edge of the back side of the exterior sleeve, aligning the raw edges, and baste in place. **FIGURE E**

2. Install the other half of the snap on the front side of the exterior sleeve, centered from side to side and 1″ to 1¼″ above the top/body seam. **FIGURE F**

3. Insert the exterior sleeve inside the lining, right sides together, aligning the raw upper edges of both. Pin and sew together around the entire upper edge, securing the tab as well. **FIGURE G**

4. Pull the exterior out through the opening at the bottom of the lining. Sew the opening in the lining closed with a blind stitch or by ironing the raw edges in to the wrong side and top-stitching close to the edge. Push the lining inside the exterior sleeve. Press the entire piece nice and flat.

Suggestions

• Personalize your sleeves with some hand-sewing details, trim, or patchwork.

• Make a pocket on the exterior for accessories like earbuds, cables, and charger.

• Quilt the exterior layer for a fun, sturdy look.

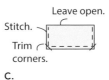

Leave open.

Stitch.

Trim corners.

C.

Open side of fabric

½″ from edge

D.

Baste.

Back side of exterior

E.

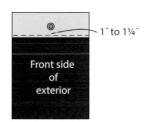

1″ to 1¼″

Front side of exterior

F.

Opening for turning

G.

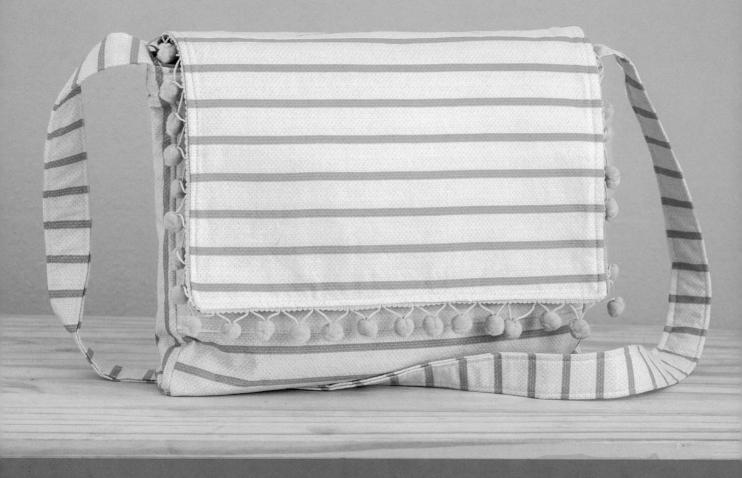

made to sell

TRIMMED KID'S MESSENGER BAG

Finished size: 12½″ wide × 9¾″ high × 2″ deep

Something about the shape of a boxy messenger bag is so appealing. Is it the nostalgia of school days, or that wearing one makes us feel like we are ready for an important adventure? This design is sure to get your customers excited. The adjustable strap is ideal if you plan on selling to kids and tweens. The younger crowd will feel especially important and stylish using this bag, which is a perfect size for their special notebooks and slim books. It uses two ½-yard pieces of fabric, and the whole project comes together fast and easy.

made to sell

❋ Lighting setup: Natural light from a window; a black foam core board blocks the reflection from the hot sun; the bag on a high dresser worked best for light at the time of shooting.

made to sell

FABRIC: For this fun bag, I used some Patty Young Textured Basics Stripes in Teal from Michael Miller Fabrics for the exterior and a solid pink canvas for the lining.

Supplies

Quilting-weight cotton, home-decor–weight fabric, and canvas are all acceptable to use for this project. If you are making multiples, plan your materials and cutting based on the number of items you are making to use your fabric efficiently.

- ½ yard fabric, at least 44″ wide, for exterior*

- ½ yard fabric, at least 44″ wide, for lining

- 1 yard of trim (pompoms, crochet trim, rickrack, or piping)

- 1 yard of lightweight fusible interfacing, 20″ wide (I use Pellon 931TD), if using quilting-weight cotton

- *Optional:* 2 D-rings 1¼″ wide for adjustable strap

* For the efficient use of fabric, pieces are cut in different directions. Consider choosing fabric without a strong directional design. Otherwise, you will need a little more fabric so that the side panels match the rest of the bag.

If your fabric is narrower than 44″, the only change you need to make is to cut a shorter pocket and strap.

Construction

Seam allowances are ¼″ unless otherwise noted.

PREPARE THE PIECES

1. If you are using quilting-weight cotton, follow the manufacturer's instructions to fuse interfacing to the wrong side of both the exterior and lining fabric pieces. Heavier-weight fabrics like canvas or duck cloth do not need interfacing, which will save you some steps. Use your judgment to determine if the weight of a home-decor fabric would benefit from interfacing.

2. Cut the fused exterior fabric into the following pieces according to the cutting layout below:

    1 piece 5″ × 44″ for the strap

    1 piece 13″ × 22″ for the exterior body

    1 piece 13″ × 10″ for the exterior flap

    1 piece 13″ × 7″ for the pocket

    2 pieces 2½″ × 10¼″ for the exterior sides

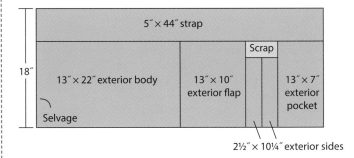

Tip

A project like this that uses the majority of the piece of fabric is the perfect occasion to save time by interfacing the whole piece of fabric instead of cutting out separate interfacing pieces.

3. Cut the fused lining fabric into the following pieces according to the cutting layout below:

 1 piece 13″ × 22″ for the lining body

 1 piece 13″ × 10″ for the flap lining

 2 pieces 2½″ × 10¼″ for the lining sides

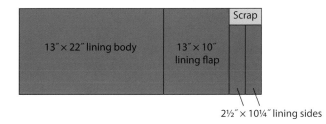

2½″ × 10¼″ lining sides

MAKE THE STRAP AND POCKET

1. Fold the 5″ × 44″ strap in half lengthwise, wrong sides together, and press. Open it back up, fold the raw edges in to the center crease, and press the edges. Fold again on the center crease so the strap is 1¼″ wide.

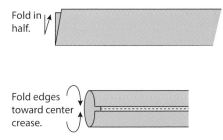

2. If you are not making the adjustable strap: Edgestitch along both long sides ⅛″ from the edge, starting with the open side, and skip Steps 3 and 4.

3. If you are making the adjustable strap: Cut a 6″ piece from the folded strap. Follow Step 2 on just this short piece.

4. Open the long strap piece back up, fold one short end ½″ to the wrong side, and press. Fold the strap back up and repeat Step 2, starting to stitch at the raw edge end of the strap, and pivoting at the end you just folded in.

5. Fold and press the upper 13″ edge of the 13″ × 7″ pocket piece over ¼″ and then ½″ to the wrong side. With the wrong side up, topstitch across the top of the pocket through all 3 layers close to the inner folded edge. This will be the upper edge of the pocket.

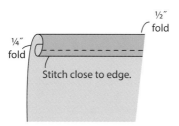

½″ fold

¼″ fold

Stitch close to edge.

6. Determine which short end of the 13″ × 22″ exterior body piece will be the front of your bag (this will be covered by the pocket and the flap eventually). Pin the bottom edge of the 13″ × 7″ pocket piece 8″ away from the upper edge of the exterior body as shown, both right sides together. Sew through both layers along the raw bottom edge of the pocket.

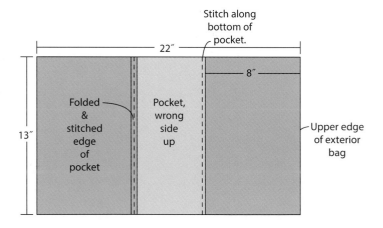

Stitch along bottom of pocket.

22″

8″

Folded & stitched edge of pocket

Pocket, wrong side up

13″

Upper edge of exterior bag

7. Fold the pocket up toward the upper edge of the body and press. Topstitch along the bottom of the pocket ¼″ from the seam.

Pocket Dividers (*optional*)

A nice way to upgrade your bag is to stitch some pocket dividers at this point. Using chalk or a disappearing-ink pen, find the center of the pocket and mark vertical lines at the center point and over in 1″ increments for as many divisions as you'd like. Stitch on the lines to make pen or pencil pockets.

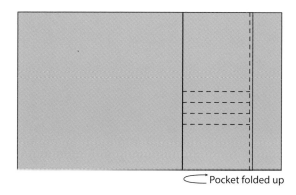

Pocket folded up

ASSEMBLE THE BAG

1. Pin the exterior body piece around 3 sides of a 2½″ × 10¼″ exterior side piece, right sides together, first pinning the top 2 corners, then the bottom 2 corners, then along the sides as needed. Make a small clip in the seam allowance of the body, if needed, to go around the bottom corners. Sew down the side, pivot, sew across the bottom edge, pivot, and sew up the other side.

2. Repeat Step 1 to pin and stitch the remaining exterior side piece to the opposite end of the exterior body.

3. Repeat Steps 1 and 2 to sew the lining side pieces to the lining body, but make sure to *leave a 4″ opening* on one of the sides for turning later.

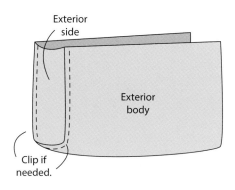

Exterior side

Exterior body

Clip if needed.

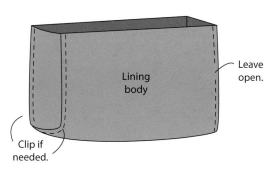

Leave open.

Lining body

Clip if needed.

MAKE THE FLAP

1. Pin and baste the trim to the right side of the exterior flap as shown, with a ¼″ seam allowance, around both 10″ sides and the bottom of the flap. If using pompom trim, make sure the balls are toward the center of the flap.

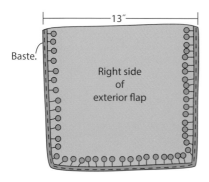

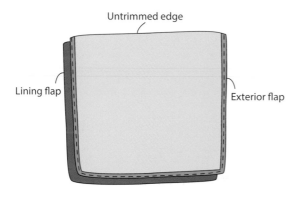

2. Pin the exterior flap and lining flap right sides together, being careful not to catch any dangling trim. Sew around the 3 trimmed sides, stitching on top of the basting.

3. Turn the flap right side out and press flat. Topstitch around the 3 trimmed sides.

ATTACH THE STRAP

1. If you are not making an adjustable strap: Center the raw ends of the strap on the sides of the assembled exterior bag body, right sides together, and pin in place. Make sure the strap is not twisted. Baste in place along the upper edge of the bag ⅛″ from the ends of the straps. Then skip to Sew the Lining and Exterior, Step 1 (page 107).

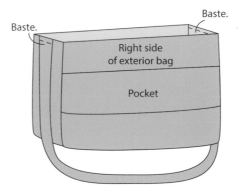

2. If you are making an adjustable strap: Wrap the 6″ strap around the flat side of 2 D-rings so the ends of the strap meet. Sew the strap together as close as possible to the D-rings to make a tab. An invisible zipper foot works well for this.

3. Pin the raw ends of the D-ring tab to one side of the assembled exterior bag body, right sides together. Baste in place ⅛″ from the upper edge.

4. Pin one end of the long strap to the opposite side of the assembled exterior bag body, right sides together. Baste in place ⅛″ from the upper edge.

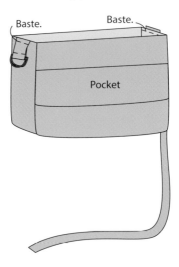

Baste.

Baste.

Pocket

SEW THE LINING AND EXTERIOR

1. Baste the assembled flap in place as shown at the upper edge of the assembled bag body, right sides together, on the back side without the pocket.

2. Place the exterior bag body (with pocket, flap, and strap attached) inside the bag lining, right sides together.

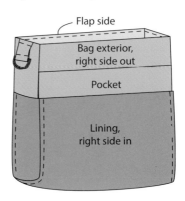

Flap side

Bag exterior, right side out

Pocket

Lining, right side in

3. Align and pin together at the side seams. Sew together around the upper raw edge. Turn the bag right side out through the side opening and then push the lining back inside the exterior. Check your seams to make sure the top edge looks nice and straight. Pull the lining back out and either hand sew the opening closed with a blind stitch or press the raw edges under and topstitch the opening closed by machine as close to the edge as possible.

4. Press the entire bag. Topstitch ⅛″ to ¼″ from the edge all the way around the upper edge of the bag.

Suggestions

• Adding some fun hardware, patchwork, and bits of leather or suede are all clever ways to spruce up this bag.

• You can eliminate the trim at the flap and use a weathered canvas to make this bag appealing to men—a handmade market that is growing quickly.

• Consider widening the sides to make the bag roomier for adults to carry more. This would mean the pattern pieces would not fit perfectly on ½ yard of fabric, but it may be worth it to improve the bag to your liking.

made to sell

HALF-SQUARE TRIANGLE QUILT

Finished quilt: *36″ × 48″* | **Finished block:** *6″ × 6″*

Handmade quilts are treasured for their beauty and detail. Nothing is cozier than reading a good book under a lovely quilt. But the time and effort it takes to create them can quickly make them too pricey for most of your customers unless you really devalue *your* time. Using a clever and fun trick to make many half-square triangles at once, you can give your customers what they want at a price that both of you will be happy about. This size is for a baby or a small lap quilt, but you can play around and make it larger to suit your needs.

Supplies

Quilting-weight fabric is recommended. If you are making multiples, plan your materials and cutting based on the number of items you are making to use your fabric efficiently. You can either prewash or not for a quilt, but if you do, make sure you wash all the fabrics before you begin.

- ⅞ yard main quilting cotton*

- ⅞ yard contrast quilting cotton*

- 1½ yards cotton batting, 45″ wide

- 1½ yards backing fabric (This can be pieced together, if you prefer, but is more effort.)

- ⅜ yard quilting cotton* for straight-grain, double-fold binding (If using premade binding, you will need 5¼ yards to bind the quilt with enough to easily join the ends.)

* See Note (page 110)

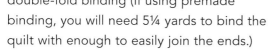

* Lighting setup: Near the back wall, natural light from a window with partially closed sheer curtains skims across the quilt to show the quilting; a white foam core board (not seen) bounces a bit of light for even lighting.

FABRIC: I used colorful, gender-neutral fabric from Timeless Treasures for this quilt. The leaf print fabric is Matilda Leaves by Alice Kennedy, and the yellow fabric is Rain Basic. Binding in Monaluna's Stripey Red adds extra pop and ties in the red in the leaves.

NOTE

The quilt in the size given requires exactly 28″ × 42″ of each fabric for the top. If you are making this quilt from fabric in your stash, or are determining yardage to make multiple quilts from the same 2 fabrics, this is the exact amount needed.

If you are purchasing single cuts of fabric, buy ⅞ yard of each. Even if prewashed and/or with selvages trimmed off, 44″-wide quilting cotton should yield an adequate piece.

If your fabric doesn't yield a 42″ usable width of fabric (WOF), divide the width by 3 to determine the largest square you can cut across the WOF. Round down to the nearest ⅛″ for ease of cutting. Your finished quilt will be smaller as a result.

Construction

Seam allowances are ¼″ unless otherwise noted.

MAKE THE HALF-SQUARE TRIANGLES

I first saw this method done by Lindsay Connor of the blog LindsaySews. (Thanks so much for letting me share your method, Lindsay!)

1. Trim the selvages and square up the main and contrast fabrics, if needed. Cut the main and contrast fabrics each into 6 squares 14″ × 14″.

14″ x 14″	14″ x 14″	14″ x 14″
14″ x 14″	14″ x 14″	14″ x 14″

2. On the wrong side of all 6 squares of one fabric, use a straightedge to draw a line diagonally from corner to corner. Then draw another line in the opposite direction to create an X across the square. I pick which fabric to mark based on which will show the drawn line the best.

3. Pin each marked square to an unmarked square, right sides together.

4. Using the X as a guide, sew the 2 squares together ¼″ from either side of the drawn lines. This means you will sew 4 lines—2 on either side of the X lines.

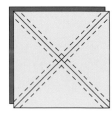

5. Using a rotary cutter and ruler, cut the square in half horizontally through the center of the X. Without moving the fabric, cut the square in half vertically through the X again. Now you have 4 pieces that have a diagonal line through them and stitches on either side of the line. Cut on both drawn lines, and like magic you will now have 8 half-square triangle blocks. Press the seam allowances either open or toward the darker fabric, as you prefer.

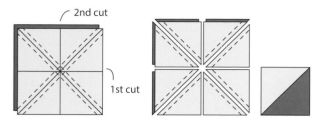

6. Repeat Steps 4 and 5 with the remaining pairs to make a total of 48 half-square triangle blocks. Trim your blocks to square them up to 6½˝ × 6½˝ unfinished, if needed.

CONSTRUCT THE QUILT TOP

1. It's time to have some fun creating your quilt top. Arrange the half-square triangle blocks in 8 rows of 6 blocks.

The 2 different layouts (at right) both use 48 half-square triangle blocks, but you can work out your own arrangement in many other ways also. The first shows the quilt as photographed (page 108).

Use a design wall or other large, flat, movable surface nearby to decide on your arrangement and help you stay organized.

2. Sew the blocks together into rows or columns; then sew the rows or columns together to make the quilt top.

Create a system for sewing together the half-square triangle blocks that will be efficient for you. I usually turn the bottom row up over the second-to-last row and then chain piece the blocks together in columns. This makes the process quick and creates fewer threads to cut. Cutting threads can take a lot of time when piecing a quilt top.

Stop to press your seams only when you have to (when you're ready to sew rows or columns together, for example) so you don't break your piecing rhythm.

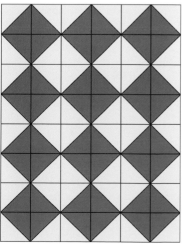

3. Press the finished quilt top and clip any stray threads.

4. Fortunately, a quilt this size will fit fine on standard-width quilting cotton for the backing, if you want to save some time; but a pieced quilt backing is a fun way to personalize your quilt and get the correct width without having to buy extrawide fabric. Cut the quilt backing and batting at least 2″ bigger in each direction than your quilt top (that is, the width of the quilt top + 4″ × the length of your quilt top + 4″).

5. Layer the backing right side down, the batting, and the quilt top right side up on a large flat surface. Smooth out any wrinkles. Baste using thread, pins, or safety pins (my preferred method) to hold the layers together. If pin-basting, place pins about a hand's width apart in a grid.

6. Quilt with either a walking foot or a free-motion foot. Check the batting manufacturer's recommendations on how far apart to space the quilting lines. Consider the trade-off between the time that quilting takes and the cost of the quilt. I usually quilt straight lines that echo the seams of the quilt top using the walking foot. Stitching in the ditch works, too, if you do it well.

7. Bind the quilt using your desired method.

Stand back to admire your beautiful creation!

Suggestions

• For a more varied look, choose 1 main fabric and 3 (or 6) other fabrics, pairing 1 main fabric and a different contrast fabric square for each half-square triangle block. That would make for even more visual interest when choosing the layout below.

• You can make many quilts by making lots of half-square triangle blocks at once. You don't have to stick to just the size I suggested either. Refer to the All-in-One Quilter's Reference Tool (by C&T Publishing) for the standard sizes of larger quilts and the number of blocks needed. For example, a lap quilt or afghan is about twice the width of this baby quilt, so start with 24 fabric squares 14″ × 14″. This will take longer to make, but you can charge more for the larger size.

PROJECTS THAT ARE
Great Sellers

There are certain items you always want to have in your shop. These are your best sellers. After you have sewn and sold a few of them, you will be able to easily sew a bunch all at once. Appealing to anyone, these best sellers are sure to move out of your shop quickly to find a happy new home.

made to sell

✳ In this section, you'll see the projects as you might use them for promotion—business cards, flyers, mailers, and so on. Compare the photos with the ones used for online sales and notice how they are different.

made to sell

BABY SET

Finished bib: *9″ × 8″* | **Finished burp cloth:** *9½″ × 17½″*

Handmade sets for baby are practically irresistible. Shoppers love to buy them for gifts and for their own little ones. So, so sweet. These instructions are for a patchwork bib and burp cloth. Consider expanding your set to include a blanket, bonnet, diaper wallet, and changing mat, all using the same easy patchwork to tie it all together.

Supplies

Quilting-weight cotton fabrics are recommended, unless specified otherwise. If you are making multiples, plan your materials and cutting based on the number of items you are making to use your fabric efficiently. The cut sizes listed assume an accurate ¼″ seam allowance.

- 1 strip 2½″ × at least 17½″ each of 5 different fabrics*

- ⅓ yard cotton chenille**

- 1 piece 10″ × 18″ cotton for backing of burp cloth

- ⅞ yard cotton twill tape or ribbon, 1¼″ wide, for the bib ties

- 1½ yards of trim, such as lace or rickrack

* Cut these from your scraps, or buy bundles of precut, coordinated 2½″-wide strips of fabric called jelly rolls or roll-ups. Each bundle has about 40 strips 2½″ × 40″, which would make 16 of these baby sets.

** Cotton chenille is recommended, but terry cloth or even quilting-weight cotton with a layer of flannel or cotton batting behind it will work well too.

made to sell

✳ When you create blog posts that use photos showing your products in use, you can let the photo carry your message. Keep posts current and fresh.

FABRIC: I wanted a simple and nostalgic print for this project. I used Robert Kaufman's 1930s reproduction fabric Grandma's Garden (by Darlene Zimmerman).

To make 16 sets:

- 1 jelly roll

- 3⅓ yards chenille

  Cut 8 strips 10″ × WOF; subcut into 18″ pieces.

  Cut the remaining fabric into 16 bib backs, 4 bibs across the WOF × 4 bibs along the remaining length.

- 2⅛ yards cotton

  Cut 4 strips 18″ × WOF; subcut into 10″ strips.

- 14 yards twill tape or ribbon

- 24 yards trim

Construction

Seam allowances are ¼″ unless otherwise noted.

PREPARE THE PIECES

1. Cut each 2½″-wide strip into 1 strip 2½″ × 7½″ and 1 strip 2½″ × 10″.

2. From the cotton chenille, cut 1 piece 10″ × 18″ for the front of the burp cloth. Copy or trace the Bib pattern piece (pullout page P1) and use it to cut 1 bib back from the remaining cotton chenille.

3. Cut the twill tape or ribbon for the bib ties into 2 equal pieces. Press and fold 1 raw end of each tie over ¼″ to the wrong side, twice. Stitch along the fold to finish the end of each tie.

Faster option: Skip the folding, pressing, and stitching and seal one end of each tie with Fray Check.

MAKE THE PATCHWORK

1. Arrange the 5 longer strips side-by-side as you like, paying attention to color and print. Sew the strips right sides together along the long edges and press the seam allowances open to make a strip set. **FIGURE A**

2. Arrange the 5 shorter strips in a different order from the strips in Step 1. Repeat Step 1 to sew and press the strips. **FIGURE B**

3. Using a rotary cutter and wide, gridded ruler, cut the strip sets perpendicular to the seams into 2½″ × 10½″ segments. The first strip set should make 4 patchwork strips and the second strip set should make 3. **FIGURE C**

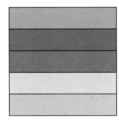

A.

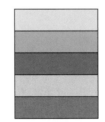

B.

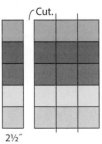

C.

MAKE THE BIB

1. Arrange 2 patchwork strips from strip set 1, and 2 from strip set 2 as shown, alternating the strips so that the same fabrics do not touch. Sew the strips, right sides together, pinning at the intersections so the seams match up. Press. **FIGURE D**

2. Place the Bib pattern piece (pullout page P1) on the right side of the patchwork and cut out 1 bib front. **FIGURE E**

3. Baste the trim around the outer edge of the patchwork bib, making sure the decorative edge of the trim is pointing toward the center of the bib. Baste the raw end of a bib tie as shown to the 2 flat upper edges of the bib, right sides together. **FIGURE F**

4. Knot the bib tie ends together loosely and pin them down in the center of the front. Pin the chenille bib back and the patchwork bib front right sides together, aligning all the raw edges and making sure the ties are away from the edges.

Using the basting as your guide, sew the 2 layers together but leave a 3″ opening on the side. Trim the corners and clip the curves. **FIGURE G**

5. Turn the bib right side out through the opening. Use a chopstick to poke out the corners; then iron nice and flat. Fold and press the seam allowances at the opening under. I like to use a strip of fusible web to close up the opening. This will ensure that the opening looks nice and neat and is practically unnoticeable. Measure the opening and cut a piece of fusible web to fit. Fuse in place according to the directions on the package. Topstitch all around the bib ⅛″ from the edge, which will also stitch the opening closed.

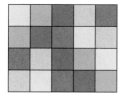

D.

E.

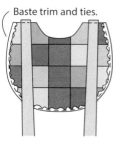

Baste trim and ties.

F.

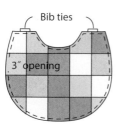

Bib ties

3″ opening

G.

MAKE THE BURP CLOTH

1. Arrange 2 patchwork strips from strip set 1, and 1 from strip set 2, as shown. Sew all 3 strips right sides together. Press. **FIGURE H**

2. Baste trim along both long edges of the patchwork, right sides together, with the decorative edge of the trim facing in toward the center. Fold and press the raw edges of the patchwork under at the basting so the trim points out. **FIGURE I**

3. Fold the 10″ × 18″ chenille burp cloth piece in half through the length to mark the center. With both pieces right side up, pin the trimmed patchwork, centered, onto the chenille piece, aligning the raw edges at the top and bottom. Sew the patchwork to the chenille close to the folded edge. **FIGURE J**

4. Pin the 10″ × 18″ burp cloth backing and chenille/patchwork top, right sides together. Sew together around the outside edge, but leave a 3″ opening on one of the sides.

5. Trim the corners. Turn the burp cloth right side out and poke out the corners with a chopstick. Iron nice and flat, and fold and press the seam allowances at the opening to the inside.

6. Topstitch around the perimeter ⅛″ from the edge, closing up the opening as well. Sew through both layers along the long edges of the patchwork, using the stitches from Step 3 as a guide. These 2 final lines of stitching will help the burp cloth fold neatly into thirds, framing the patchwork.

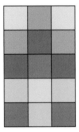

H.

Baste.

I.

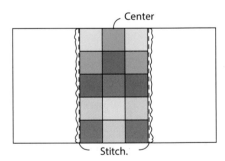

Center

Stitch.

J.

Suggestions

- If you want to make these faster, skip the patchwork and just use pieces of fabric to make the front of the bib and burp cloth. For the bib, cut a piece 8½″ × 10″, and for the burp cloth, 6½″ × 10″.

- Experiment with the ties if you don't like the cotton twill. Ties that match your bib fabric would be cute.

- Double or triple the length given for the 2½″-wide fabric strips and make more than one set at a time.

made to sell

New Year's Resolution #87
Get Organized

handy organizer
with pockets

gingercake
www.gingercake.com

$20

HANDY ORGANIZER

Finished organizer: 12¾″ × 9¼″ (opened), 6″ wide × 9¼″ high × ¾″ deep (closed)

I have been sewing and gifting versions of this organizer for years. It is always a hit with people of all ages. The organizer is easy to sew and it is fun to mix the fabrics together to make a really stylish and useful accessory. This version has an exterior pocket, optional fabric tie, and extra space on the inside. Feel free to add more pockets or take it down to a minimum for extra-fast construction.

Supplies

Quilting-weight fabric is used in my version, but replacing some fabrics with canvas or duck cloth would look great and eliminate some fusible interfacing. If you are making multiples, plan your materials and cutting based on the number of items you are making to use your fabric efficiently.

- 1 piece at least 13½″ × 20″ of fabric 1
- 1 piece at least 13½″ × 17½″ of fabric 2
- 1 piece at least 13½″ × 9″ of fabric 3
- 1⅛ yards fusible interfacing, 20″ wide
- 1 piece 13½″ × 10″ batting

Stock Your Shelves

To make 4:

- ⅞ yard of fabric 1

  Cut 2 strips 13½″ × WOF; subcut into 20″ strips.

- ⅞ yard of fabric 2

  Cut 2 strips 13½″ × WOF; subcut into 4 strips 10″ wide and 4 strips 7¾″ wide.

- ½ yard of fabric 3

  Cut pieces along the length.

- 3½ yards of 20″-wide interfacing

- 20″ × 27″ piece of batting (or equivalent)

made to sell

✳ Draw people into your booth with a sign that will catch customers' eyes. Make it graphic and easy to see.

FABRIC: This organizer was made using Timeless Treasures' Writing by Samarra Khaja, their Sketch Basic in Sky, and Ann Kelle's Ovals from Robert Kaufman.

Construction

Seam allowances are ⅜″ unless otherwise noted. Use a walking foot to make it easier to sew the layers together.

PREPARE THE PIECES

1. Cut fabric 1 into 2 pieces 13½″ × 10″ for the lining and the outer pocket.

- Cut fabric 2 into 1 piece 13½″ × 10″ for the exterior and 1 piece 13½″ × 7¾″ for the large inner pocket.

- Cut fabric 3 into 1 piece 13½″ × 5¼″ for the small inner pocket and 2 pieces 2″ × 13½″ for the ties.

2. Cut interfacing to fit all fabric pieces *except the 2 ties*. Follow the manufacturer's instructions to fuse interfacing to the wrong side of the corresponding fabric pieces.

3. Fold and press 1 short end of a tie ½″ to the wrong side. Then press the tie in half lengthwise, wrong sides together. Open it back up and then press both long raw edges in to the center crease. Fold back up along the center to make a tie ½″ wide. Repeat with the other tie. **FIGURES A, B, C, & D**

4. Machine stitch each tie closed, ⅛″ from the folded edge. **FIGURE E**

CONSTRUCT THE POCKETS

1. Fold and press the upper long edge of the large inner pocket over ½″ to the wrong side twice.

2. Working with the wrong side up, edgestitch along the fold as close to the outer edge of the pocket as possible.

3. Repeat Steps 1 and 2 with the small inner pocket

4. Fold the exterior pocket in half, right sides together, along the 10″ edge as shown. Pin and sew closed, using a ¼″ seam allowance, to make a tube. **FIGURE F**

5. Finger-press the seam allowances open and turn the tube right side out. Press it flat with the seam running down the center. Topstitch along both outer edges. **FIGURE G**

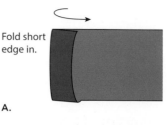

Fold short edge in.

A.

Fold in half.

B.

Fold edges toward center crease.

C.

Fold in half again.

Original crease

D.

E.

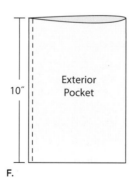

10″

Exterior Pocket

F.

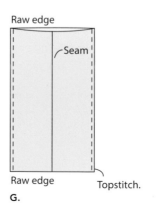

Raw edge

Seam

Raw edge

Topstitch.

G.

ASSEMBLE THE LAYERS

1. Mark the center along one long edge of the 13½″ × 10″ exterior piece. Mark a line down the center of the pocket. Place the exterior pocket, seam side down, on the exterior piece, right side up, aligning the centers. Topstitch on the line to attach the pocket. *Optional:* Baste the raw edges of the pocket to the exterior piece. **FIGURE H**

2. Layer the batting, the 13½″ × 10″ lining piece, the large inner pocket, and the small inner pocket, with all fabrics right side up and aligned at the bottom raw edges. Pin the ties in place along the sides, aligning the raw edges, 5″ from the bottom.

3. Pin together or baste around the perimeter (or at the very least, across each tie) with a ⅛″ seam allowance. **FIGURE I**

FINISH IT UP

1. Layer the interior and exterior, right sides together, with the exterior on the top. Pin all around. Sew around the perimeter *using a ⅜″ seam allowance*, and leave an opening for turning. **FIGURE J**

2. Trim the corners and trim the batting in the seam allowances down.

3. Turn the organizer right side out, poke out the corners with a chopstick, and press it flat. For the opening, press the raw edges under to match the seams. Use a small strip of fusible web or a blind stitch to close up the opening.

4. Topstitch around the perimeter, ¼″ to ⅛″ from the edge. **FIGURE K**

5. To make the pen/pencil pocket in the center of the organizer, sew ⅜″ away from either side of the center seam on the exterior pocket. This also makes it easy to fold the organizer in half. **FIGURE K**

Suggestions

• You can alter this organizer in so many ways. For the closure, use a button and elastic loop, or make a tab for a hook-and-loop tape or magnetic snap closure.

• For sales, include a 5″ × 8″ pad of paper and a nice pen or pencil. Don't forget to include these materials when determining your price.

• Mix up the fabric combinations and add trim or embroidery to give your pieces a special look.

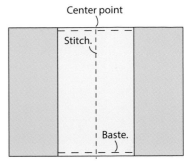

H.

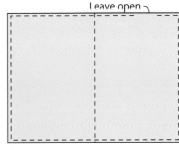

I

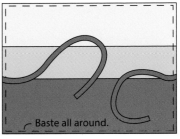

J.

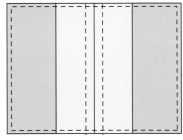

K.

Are You Ready for Summer?

The "Great Big Tote" is perfect for a lovely day at the beach.

This tote is a must-have for summer.

With sturdy handles and a roomy pocket, this tote will carry all of your beachy accessories. And the colorful, fresh print on this bag is versatile enough to carry you from the waterfront to a bbq!

made to sell

GREAT BIG TOTE

Finished tote: 12½″ wide × 16″ high × 7″ deep

This tote is great for carrying tons of stuff. Your customers will imagine themselves taking it to a picnic, to the beach, or to the farmers' market. This tote can handle it all. The special ingredient is painter's drop cloth canvas fabric for the lining, the base, and the handles. The natural color of the canvas, its sturdiness, and its loose weave give the bag a casual yet stylish look. Canvas drop cloths can be found in the paint section of home improvement stores. Wash them once or twice before you begin sewing to soften the fabric.

Supplies

If you are making multiples, plan your materials and cutting based on the number of items you are making to use your fabric efficiently.

- ⅞ yard canvas, 55″ wide, or 1 piece 28″ × 52″ canvas drop cloth
- ½ yard cotton fabric (quilting weight or home-decor weight)
- ¼ yard contrasting fabric for pocket
- 1¼ yards fusible interfacing, 20″ wide

* Postcards are multipurpose—mail them to people who don't use email and slip them in with purchases as a reminder. Remember to use both sides for your message.

FABRIC: I used Art Gallery Fabrics' lovely Tule line by Leah Duncan for this big tote.

Construction

Seam allowances are ¼″ unless otherwise noted.

PREPARE THE PIECES

1. Cut the canvas fabric or drop cloth into the following pieces, using the cutting layout below as a guide:

   1 piece 20″ × 40″ for the lining body

   1 piece 20″ × 12″ for the exterior base

   2 pieces 4″ × 48″ for the handles

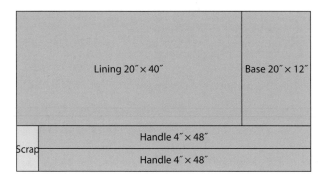

2. Cut the pocket fabric into 2 pieces 8″ × 18″.

3. Cut the cotton fabric into 2 pieces 20″ × 15″.

4. Cut the interfacing into the following pieces:

   2 pieces 20″ × 15″

   2 pieces 8″ × 9″

5. Follow the manufacturer's instructions to fuse the 20″ × 15″ interfacing pieces to the wrong side of the corresponding cotton pieces.

6. Fold the 8″ × 18″ pocket pieces in half widthwise as shown and press to mark a center crease. Open up the creased pieces. Follow the manufacturer's instructions to fuse the 8″ × 9″ interfacing pieces to the wrong side of each half of the pockets that will be the front.

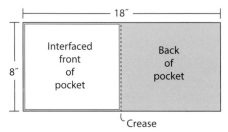

MAKE THE HANDLES AND POCKETS

1. Fold and press 1 handle piece in half lengthwise, wrong sides together. Open it back up and then press both long raw edges in to the center crease. Fold back up along the center to make a handle 1″ wide. Repeat with the other handle. Machine stitch each handle closed, ⅛″ from the folded edge; then stitch along the other long sides ⅛″ from the edge.

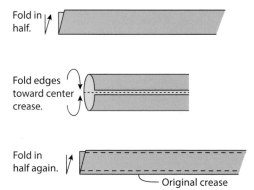

2. Fold the pocket pieces wrong sides together along the center creases. Topstitch across both folded edges.

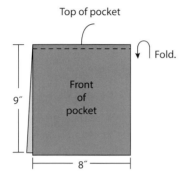

EXTERIOR ASSEMBLY

1. Mark the center of the 20˝ × 15˝ exterior body pieces along the long bottom edge. Mark the center of the 8˝ × 9˝ pockets along the bottom raw edge. Center a pocket on each exterior bag piece, aligning the raw edges at the bottom. Baste in place on the sides.

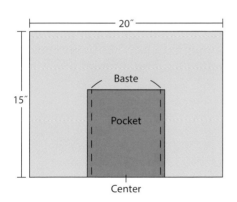

2. Pin the raw edges of a handle to an exterior body piece, centered over one side of the pocket as shown, aligning the raw edges at the bottom. Use a long ruler to guide the handle straight up from the pocket sides to the top of the exterior body. Pin in place, using 2 pins 1˝ from the top edge to mark where to stop sewing. Make sure the handle is not twisted. Repeat this step with the other handle and exterior body piece.

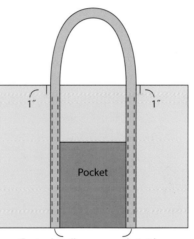

Center handles over pocket sides.

3. Following the previous lines of top stitching on either side of the handle, sew the handle to the exterior bag piece on both sides of the pocket, making sure to stop 1˝ from the top edge of the body. Repeat with the other exterior body and handle.

4. Sew one long edge of the 12″ × 20″ canvas base to 1 exterior body piece, right sides together, with a ½″ seam allowance. Press (with an iron, or just finger-press as the canvas is easy to manipulate) the seam allowance down toward the canvas and topstitch on the canvas ¼″ from the seam. Repeat this step to sew the other exterior body piece to the opposite side of the base.

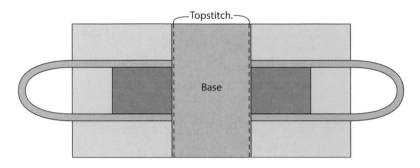

5. The 20″ × 40″ canvas lining should be the same size as the exterior you just finished assembling. Quickly check to make sure they match before you sew up the sides of the exterior. If not, trim the larger piece to match the smaller.

6. Fold the assembled exterior right sides together, making sure the seams between the base and the body meet. Pin the 2 sides together and sew. Press. Turn the exterior right side out and poke the corners out with a chopstick.

MAKE THE LINING

1. Fold the 20″ × 40″ canvas lining in half and sew the side seams, leaving a 4″ gap on one side for turning. Press.

2. Fold the handles down toward the pockets and pin in place temporarily. Insert the exterior inside the lining, right sides together. Align the side seams and pin around the top raw edges, beginning at the side seams. Sew the exterior and lining together with a ½″ seam allowance.

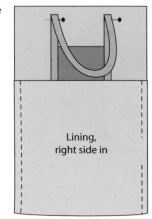

3. Pull the bag right side out through the opening in the lining.

4. Hand sew the lining closed with a blind stitch or by pressing the seam allowances to the wrong side; topstitch close to the edge.

5. Push the lining inside the bag and use a chopstick to push the corners of the lining all the way into the corner of the exterior. Unpin the handles and pull them up above the bag. Press the bag well, especially around the upper edge.

6. Topstitch all around the opening of the tote ¼″ from the edge, stitching over the handles so they are secured.

MAKE THE BOXED CORNERS

A fun feature of the great big tote is the exterior view of the bottom corners. They give the tote extra strength and structure.

1. Working from the side of the bag, flatten the base out into a triangle with the side seam running down the middle, making sure to catch both the exterior and the lining (just like making a boxed corner from the inside of a bag). Measure 3½″ in from the tip of the triangle and mark a line across the base that should measure 7″ across. Pin and sew on the line.

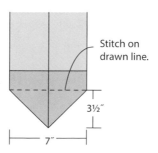

Stitch on drawn line.

3½″

7″

2. Fold the triangle up against the side of the bag, lining up the tip with the side seam. Topstitch the upper sides of the triangle onto the side of the bag. To make it easier to avoid catching the other side of the bag in the stitching, use the free-arm feature on your sewing machine (check the owner's manual if you're not sure what to do).

You may need to sew from the triangle tip down on each side.

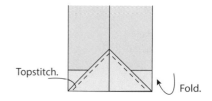

Topstitch.

Fold.

3. Press the bag well.

Suggestions

- This great big tote looks fantastic in a big, bold fabric. Experiment with fabrics to find a combination you like.

- Add extra pockets to the interior or remove the exterior pocket if you would like.

- Experiment with sizes. A smaller size would also be useful and a great seller.

made to sell

PROFESSIONAL AND PERFECT REVERSIBLE PILLOW COVERS

SUGGESTED PRICE POINT

$15 TO **$35**

(DEPENDING ON HOW MUCH DETAIL YOU PUT INTO THE PILLOW FRONTS)

Finished pillow covers: 16″ × 16″

When I bought these invisible zippers at the store, the saleslady asked, "What are you making?" I answered, "Pillow covers." And she said, "With these? I guess you want them to look perfect, huh? Like a professional?" I just nodded and thought, Oh, yes—perfect *and* professional—that *is* what I want.

Invisible zippers on the side of your pillow covers make them look so nice, and installing them is easy with a little practice.

Pillows are a good addition to your craft booth because they draw people in with their size and comfortable shape. Give your customers the option of buying them with or without the pillow form. When you need extra space in your booth, take the pillow forms out of the covers. When you need to fill up some space later in the day, put the forms in to keep your table looking full.

Supplies

Use quilting-weight or decor-weight fabrics. Materials listed are for 1 pillow. If you are making multiples, plan your materials and cutting based on the number of items you are making to use your fabric efficiently.

- 2 pieces 16½″ × 16½″ quilting-weight or decor-weight fabric for pillow exterior

- 2 pieces 16″ × 16″ fabric for lining, such as muslin

- 1 invisible zipper, 12″–14″ long

- 1 pillow form, 16″ × 16″ square, if desired

- *Optional:* Invisible zipper foot

✳ Emails are an easy and inexpensive way to reach your customers. They are especially effective for special events, such as "1-day only" sales.

FABRIC: The fun print I used is a Robert Kaufman fabric called Remix Ovals by Ann Kelle.

Stock Your Shelves

To make 3:

• ½ yard each 2 different 54″-wide fabrics

• 1 yard 60″-wide muslin

• 3 zippers

• 3 pillow forms

Construction

Seam allowances are ¼″ unless otherwise noted.

MAKE PILLOW EXTERIORS

1. Layer the 2 exterior 16½″ × 16½″ pieces right sides together. *If your fabric has a nap or directional design, rotate 1 piece 90° so all your pieces will be oriented correctly when finished.* With a straightedge, cut both in half diagonally to make 4 triangle pieces.

2. Pin 2 different triangle pieces together on the diagonal. Sew together carefully, making sure not to stretch the bias edges. Repeat with the other 2 pieces. Press the seam allowances open.

3. Layer the pieced pillow exteriors, centered, onto the 16″ × 16″ lining squares, wrong sides together. Trim, keeping the shape square, with your rotary cutter and a straightedge so the 2 layers match perfectly.

4. If you have a serger, serge the perimeter of the 2 layers together. Otherwise, just zigzag stitch the lining and the exterior together. Now you should have 2 lined pieces.

5. Topstitch ¼″ away from both sides of the diagonal seam on all 4 pillow exteriors. Repeat with the other side of the pillow front.

ATTACH THE INVISIBLE ZIPPER

1. Read the packaging instructions carefully to install the invisible zipper. If you do not have an invisible zipper foot, just use your regular zipper foot but make sure to press (using a low setting) the teeth of the zipper away from the back side of the zipper first.

2. Open the zipper and pin it, centered, to one side of your pillow exteriors, both right sides together. Sew the zipper just between the 2 stops at either end of the zipper.

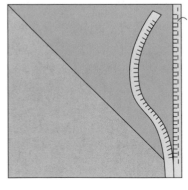

Stitch pillow front and zipper, right sides together.

3. Pin the other side of the zipper, again with right sides together, to the other pillow exterior, matching the centered zipper placement on the other piece. Sew the zipper again just between the zipper stops.

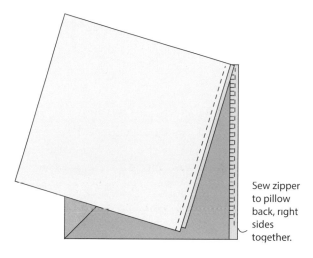

Sew zipper to pillow back, right sides together.

SEW THE PILLOW TOGETHER

1. Close up the zipper and fold the pillow fronts so they are right sides together and the edges match up. Pin the corners on the side where the zipper is already installed. You should not have sewn all the way to the ends, since we sewed only between the stops on the zipper. *The zipper ends should be pushed out and away from the fabric layers.*

2. *Important:* When the corner on the zipper side is pinned, reach underneath and unzip the zipper halfway.

3. Line up your layers again, right sides together, and pin all the way around. Start sewing at the corner where the zipper is installed. Pick up the seam where you stopped with the zipper and sew around the perimeter of the pillow, pivoting at the corners. Stop at the other end of the zipper seam.

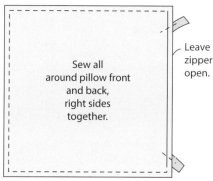

Sew all around pillow front and back, right sides together.

Leave zipper open.

FINISH IT UP

1. Clip off the corners and turn the pillow right side out. Use a chopstick to poke out the corners. Zip up the zipper and press your pillow nice and flat.

2. Unzip the zipper and insert the pillow form. Zip it up and fluff it nicely for photographs.

Suggestions

The way I made my pillow exteriors is just a suggestion. The invisible zipper is what makes this a nice pillow for sales. Experiment to find your own style when making more pillows like this.

made to sell

SLOUCH BAG

Finished bag: 15½″ × 13⅞″

This easy and stylish slouch bag can be made with several modifications. Make this bag with your own bold prints, extra pockets, and any other feature you like to see in your bags. The style has a little more structure than most bags of this type and features a fun bit of simple hardware at the shoulder strap.

Supplies

Lightweight home-decor fabric is recommended, but quilting-weight fabric is fine, too. If you are making multiples, plan your materials and cutting based on the number of items you are making to use your fabric efficiently.

- 1 piece at least 16″ × 30″ for the main exterior fabric

- 1 piece at least 13″ × 16″ for the contrasting exterior fabric

- 1 piece at least 18″ × 32″ for the lining fabric (I used painter's drop cloth canvas.)

- 2 D-rings, 1¼″ wide

- Pliers

Stock Your Shelves

To make 6:

- 2⅛ yards main fabric

  Cut 4 strips 16″ × WOF; subcut each into 3 pieces 12″ wide and 1 piece 6″ wide.

  Cut 1 strip 6″ × WOF; subcut into 2 strips 16″ long.

- 1 yard contrasting fabric

  Cut 2 strips 16″ wide; subcut into 13″-wide pieces.

- 2¾ yard 40″-wide lining fabric

  Cut 3 strips 32″ × WOF; subcut each into 2 pieces 18″ wide.

- 12 D rings

---

made to sell

✳ Use business cards that show your style. Carry them with you at all times to hand out and be sure to have plenty on hand at shows. Slip them in with purchases, too.

FABRIC: I chose to use these bold Art Gallery Fabrics because I loved the colors. They are from the Bijoux line by Bari J.

Construction

Seam allowances are ¼˝ unless otherwise noted.

PREPARE THE PIECES

1. From the main exterior fabric, cut 2 bottom exterior pieces each 12˝ × 16˝ and 1 handle piece 6˝ × 16˝.

2. Fold each bottom exterior piece in half lengthwise to 12˝ × 8˝. Copy or trace pattern A (pullout page P2) and use it to cut out the curve and dart on the folded pieces.

3. From the contrasting exterior fabric, cut 2 top exterior pieces each 6½˝ × 16˝. Fold the pieces in half crosswise to 6½˝ × 8˝. Copy or trace pattern B (pullout page P2) and use it to cut the pieces.

MAKE THE EXTERIOR BAG

1. Sew a main exterior piece and a contrasting exterior piece right sides together to make a full exterior piece. Press. If you used quilting-weight cotton and would like the extra structure, this would be the time to apply fusible interfacing.

2. Use 1 of the full exterior pieces from Step 1 as a pattern piece for the lining fabric. Trace and cut out 2 matching lining pieces.

3. Pin and sew each of the 4 darts on the 2 full exterior pieces. Press.

4. Layer the 2 full exterior pieces right sides together. Pin around the outside. Sew just the outside edges together. Press. Turn the bag right side out.

MAKE THE LINING AND ATTACH TO THE EXTERIOR

1. Pin and sew each of the 4 darts on the 2 lining pieces.

2. Layer the 2 lining pieces, right sides together. Pin and sew around just the outside edges (like you did with the exterior), but this time leave a 4˝ opening in the bottom of the bag for turning.

3. Insert the exterior bag inside the lining, right sides together. Match and pin at the side seams. Match and pin the top edges that will hold the D-rings. Sew together these top edges; zigzag stitch the seam allowance for extra stability.

4. Pin the curve on both sides of the bag opening. Instead of starting right at the top of the curve, begin sewing ½″ down to leave room for a D-ring. Stop ½″ from the top on the other side. Backstitch a couple of times at the start and stop. Repeat with the other curved side. Clip the fabric around the curves. Leave the top corners unclipped.

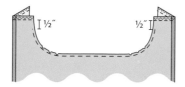

5. Using the opening at the base of the lining, pull the bag right side out, pushing the lining inside the exterior bag. Press, paying special attention to the curved top.

6. Topstitch ¼″ or less from the edge around the curved opening of the bag. When you get to the top edges, sew ⅝″ away from the top edge to leave room for the D-ring.

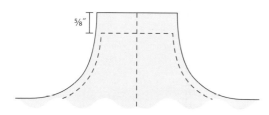

MAKE THE HANDLE AND ADD D-RINGS

1. Press both ends of the 6″ × 16″ handle fabric under ½″. Fold and press it in half lengthwise to 3″ × 15″. Open the lengthwise fold and press the raw edges in toward the center crease. Refold at the center. Topstitch the long folded edges ⅛″ from the edge; then topstitch the other long edge.

2. Loop the handle through the curved side of the D-ring. Fold the fabric back onto itself about 1″ down around the D-ring. Pin and sew the handle closed. Repeat with the other end of the handle and the other D-ring. Make sure to fold the handle fabric under to the same side on both ends so it doesn't end up twisted.

3. Use the pliers to open a D-ring about ¼″. Insert the D-ring through the opening in one of the top edges of the bag. Push your fabric over to the side and use your pliers to muscle the D-ring closed. Repeat with the other D-ring on the other top edge of the bag. Note: This may take some trial and error to get the D-ring opened and closed without too much damage to it. Be patient. You will find a method that works easily. I found that a channel lock plier is useful to close the D-ring.

Suggestions

• Insert a magnetic snap in the lining before you attach the lining and exterior together. Although the shape of the bag makes it close naturally on your shoulder, this is an upgrade that your customers may like.

• Add a pocket to the lining for extra storage. I would suggest a 7″ × 8″ size.

• Make the exterior all one fabric for a super-fast sewing project.

• Experiment with other hardware besides D-rings to attach your handle. A lot of unique hardware pieces are made specifically for bag making and would work great with this bag.

made to sell

Show Special!

FREE Zipper Pouch
with $75 purchase!

ZIPPED POUCH

Finished pouch: 8″ wide (top) / 5½″ wide (bottom) × 5¼″ high × 2½″ deep

Always a great seller and fun to make, zipped pouches are both useful and stylish. Everybody loves them. This method makes a piece that is quick and professional looking. The result is a great handmade pouch that is sure to please your customers. Feel free to change it up to make it your own.

Supplies

Quilting-weight fabric is recommended. If you are making multiples, plan your materials and cutting based on the number of items you are making to use your fabric efficiently.

- 1 piece at least 8½″ × 9″ for the main exterior fabric

- 1 piece at least 8½″ × 6″ for the base exterior fabric (I used painter's drop cloth canvas.)

- 1 piece at least 8½″ × 14″ for the lining fabric

- ½ yard of lightweight fusible interfacing, 20″ wide

- 9″ zipper

Stock Your Shelves

To make 4:

- ⅓ yard main exterior fabric

  Cut 1 strip 8½″ × WOF; subcut into 9″ lengths.

- ¼ yard base exterior fabric

  Cut 1 strip 6″ × WOF; subcut into 8½″ lengths.

- ½ yard lining fabric

  Cut 1 strip 14″ × WOF; subcut into 8½″ strips.

- 1⅝ yards interfacing

- 4 zippers

made to sell

✳ Advertise your show special with a handout that has a great photo showing people exactly what they'll get. How enticing!

FABRIC: I used another Art Gallery Fabrics print from the Tule line by Leah Duncan for this pouch.

Construction

Seam allowances are ¼″ unless otherwise noted.

PREPARE THE PIECES

1. Fuse interfacing to the back of the quilting-weight pieces.

2. Cut the 8½″ × 9″ main exterior fabric into 2 pieces each 8½″ × 4½″.

3. Cut the 8½″ × 6″ base exterior fabric into 2 pieces each 8½″ × 3″.

4. Cut the 8½″ × 14″ lining fabric into 2 pieces each 8½″ × 7″.

ASSEMBLE THE EXTERIOR

1. Sew an 8½″ × 3″ base exterior piece and an 8½″ × 4½″ main exterior piece, right sides together, along an 8½″ side. Press the seam toward the base. Topstitch on the base side ⅛″ from the seam. Repeat with the other base exterior and main exterior pieces to create 2 full exterior pieces.

2. Align the zipper, facedown, with the top edge of a full exterior piece. The right side of the exterior piece should be facing the right side of the zipper. Line up the stops on the zipper about ¼″ from each side of the exterior piece. Pin and sew the zipper on with your zipper foot.

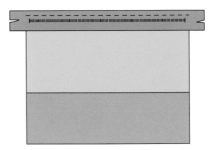

3. Turn the zipper faceup and finger-press the seam away from the zipper teeth.

4. Place the zipper and attached exterior piece facedown on top of the remaining full exterior piece. The right sides of the fabric should be facing each other, and the top edge of the zipper should be lined up with the top edge of the exterior fabric. Again, the zipper should be centered. Pin and sew together with your zipper foot.

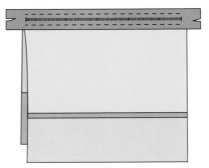

5. Finger-press the seams away from the zipper teeth.

ATTACH THE LINING

Use the seams you made attaching the zipper to the exterior as guides in attaching the lining to the wrong side of the zipper.

1. Align the 2 exterior pieces with right sides together. You should be looking at the wrong side of the zipper and the wrong side of an exterior piece.

2. Align the top edge of a lining piece (8½″ wide) with the top edge of the zipper. The lining and the zipper should both be right side facing down. The lining piece should be centered and covering up the entire zipper (except the zipper's longer ends).

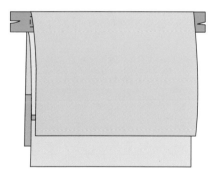

3. Pin and flip over. You will see the seam you made earlier to attach the exterior to the right side of the zipper. Use this line to guide you to sew on the first side of the lining.

4. Position the piece so the first lining side is on top again. Turn that layer of lining over so that it is right side facing up.

5. Switch the 2 exterior layers over to the other side (but still underneath the first lining piece). Now you have the last unsewn side of the zipper showing.

6. Align the remaining lining piece, right side down, with the second edge of the zipper. The zipper is also right side down.

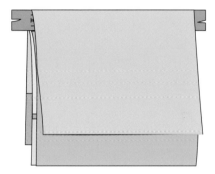

7. Pin and turn over. You should see the *other* seam where you attached the *other* side of the exterior piece to the front side of the zipper. Use that line as a guide to sew and attach the lining to the zipper.

8. Arrange the piece so that the zipper is right side up in the middle, the exterior pieces are flat on either side, and the lining pieces are flat on either side below the exterior pieces. Press the seams away from the zipper on medium heat.

SEW THE SIDES

Before you sew the sides, open the zipper about halfway.

1. Separate the exterior pieces and the lining pieces. Place the right sides of the exterior together and the right sides of the lining together. Pin. The seams that include the zipper edges should be facing toward the exterior side. The zipper is folded right sides together inside the 2 lining pieces.

2. Leave a 3″ opening at the base of the lining to turn your piece right side out. Begin sewing at one edge of the opening, and sew the perimeter of the piece (over the zipper), and then stop at the other edge of your 3″ opening.

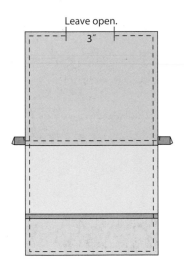

3. Trim the ends of the zipper so that they are even with the sides of the fabric.

MAKE THE GUSSET CORNERS (OPTIONAL)

1. Reach your hand into the opening in the lining and all the way through the opening in the zipper to one of the exterior corners. Flatten the corner out into a triangular shape

with the seam in the middle. Pin the layers together. Draw a line 1¼″ from the tip of the corner. Sew on the line; trim the fabric above the line.

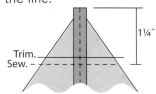

2. Repeat Step 1 with the other exterior corner and the 2 lining corners.

FINISH THE POUCH

1. If you didn't make the optional gusset corners, clip the seams at the 2 exterior corners and the 2 lining corners.

2. Using the opening in the lining, reach in and pull the piece right side out. Push the lining inside the exterior side. Use a chopstick to poke the corners of the exterior out.

3. After checking that all your seams look good and you are happy with the shape, pull the lining back out. Either blindstitch to close the opening or press under the edges of the opening and topstitch closed as close to the edges as possible. Push the lining back inside the exterior, and you are finished.

Suggestions

- This project is perfect for lots of variations. One thing I like to do is make the same pouch in 3 sizes and sell them as a set. Let the zipper sizes guide you.

- Use trim and patchwork to make the pouches more personalized, but don't get bogged down in too much detail!

- Forget the canvas base and make the exterior all one fabric.

Appendix

BUSINESS BASICS

Yes, you know this had to be here somewhere. Along with the freedom and fun of making money at something you love to do comes responsibility. Although you will be able to spend many hours sewing, it's important to remember that you also have to take care of the business side of your business.

You're In Charge

From the beginning of this book, you've been reading about what is involved in making a profession of your sewing. Now it's up to you to actually put it into practice.

Create a schedule of when you will work and try to stick to it. Of course, you have to be flexible, but committing to a schedule will work wonders for your productivity. Discuss this time with your family and make sure they understand that you are at work when you are sewing. You will find that they will respect your work time and take you more seriously.

After you commit to a schedule, try to make the most of your work time. I recently read a blog post about a sewist who plans for her sewing day all week. She makes dinner the day before (a casserole), has done the laundry and picked up the house, and has made arrangements so her kids are occupied. This means her day spent sewing is very fruitful. She can accomplish so much because she planned ahead and took care of everything that might otherwise interrupt her. You might be able to work in the evenings or on specific days of the week. The point is, it's up to you make a plan and then follow through.

Keeping Your Look Fresh

It's important to regularly evaluate the goods in your shop. It's easy to get so caught up in the details of production sewing that you forget to look at the big picture. Is your shop carrying a good mix of items? Are your prices current with other sellers? Are you looking at trends so you can create something new if needed?

If you are doing a show, a mix of handmade items is important so that your customers have a good selection to choose from. I am not talking about that trap of something for everyone, but instead, items in a modest range of prices and sizes. For example, if you are specializing in home accessories, your shop should include small things such as stacks of coasters, medium-sized things such as place mats and table runners, and large items such as big patchwork pillows. Another example would be a booth for kids having things for both girls and boys.

For your online shop, trends and popular colors are important. Evaluating current trends might give your online shop a fresh look. For example, 2013 was a great year for the color orange, feathers, and arrows. It may seem silly, but little adjustments, such as a new orange banner or adding some items using fabric with arrows to your line, will keep your shop up to date. If you do choose to make some changes, even if they are on the trendy side, make sure you do them because you like them and they work with your style. Don't do it just because everyone else is.

Inventory

Keeping track of the materials and supplies you have on hand allows you to use what you have and to know when you need to buy more.

Keeping track of what you make and what you sell will help you to plan better in the future. If you are making red, green, yellow, and purple grocery totes, keeping track of what sells best will help you to know what to make more of in the future. Knowing that you sold out of your pillow covers in the first hour of your show will let you know to make more in the future (and to price them higher). You may find that using a spreadsheet such as Excel is all you need. As your business grows, you may have to get a more detailed system.

CRAFT FAIRS AND SHOWS

To keep inventory at a show, I simply write down everything I bring and then write down everything I bring home. Candace Todd of Sparkle Power hangs a simple tag with an item description on all her handmade items before a show begins. When things sell, she snips off the tags and keeps them to review and make notes of what sold best when she gets home.

I highly recommend bringing along a friend who has the job of tracking what sells. That friend usually hangs back behind the table while you schmooze your customers. She gives out change, writes down what you sell, and packages everything up. You can either pay her some of your profit (out of your business account) or bribe her with free handmade lovelies as gifts.

ONLINE SALES

For online sales, keeping track of what sells can save you time and make you money. For example, Monica Donohue of Little Pigeon tests new lines of fabric first to see how well they sell. When one does well, she makes the investment in buying more of the fabric and makes that line part of her shop. She is not just buying and making without any sort of strategy, since that would be a waste of her resources and time. (See Interview with Monica Donohue, page 33.)

The Legal Aspects of Setting Up a Shop

You will need to look into a few things for your business to be legal, especially if you are going to operate under a name other than your own.

DOING BUSINESS AS (DBA) OR FILING A FICTITIOUS NAME STATEMENT

If you are going to be doing business under a name other than your own, you need to look into filing a Doing Business As (DBA) or Fictitious Name Statement. Fortunately, this can generally be done online, or if you want to talk to someone, check with the appropriate office for your city, county, or state. Before you do this, you should search the available databases to make sure no one else has the name you want to use.

GET A TAX ID NUMBER

Again, if you are going to be doing business under a name other than your own, you need to get a tax ID number (also known as an EIN). Fortunately, you can do this online on the IRS website.

SET UP BANK ACCOUNTS

After you have your business name and your tax ID number, it's a good idea to have a separate bank account and credit or debit card for your business. You may want to link accounts through PayPal or another payment-accepting service (see Resources, page 149).

Tip
Don't be daunted by this. Think of all the other sewists, artists, and crafters who have gone through this process. If they can do it, so can you.

HOW TO PAY SALES TAX

When you sell at a show, you'll need to find out the sales tax rules for the state, county, and maybe even city that you are in. Show management often supplies this information for the vendors.

For online sales, you generally have to charge sales tax only to people who live in your state (if you live in a state that charges sales tax). Customers from other states are required to pay their own taxes.

INCOME TAX

And of course, because you are going to be making money at this (right?), you need to consider income taxes. Basically, you need to have a way of keeping track of your income and your expenses. Your income is what you make from your sales, and your expense is all the fabric, batting, thread, interfacing, and miscellaneous sewing things you bought. If you pay a helper either to sew with you or to babysit your kids while you sew, that is also a business expense. You can do this in a variety of ways, and it is worth the effort of setting it up **before** you start selling—this will make tax time a lot simpler.

One way to easily accomplish this is through PayPal. You'll be able to accept payments online, and you can get a debit card that will draw directly from your account balance. Use this debit card to buy materials and other essentials for your business. When tax time comes, you'll be able to see your income and most of your expenses through your PayPal account.

PayPal has its limitations, and you will probably need to set up a bank account that is connected to PayPal for more flexibility. An excellent website to use is godaddy.com (see All Products > Invoicing & Payments > Online Bookkeeping) because it was created for small businesses to help owners keep track of income and expenses. It will link directly to PayPal and Etsy and show you wonderful graphs of your income versus expenses and other information. Come tax time, you can either use this well-organized earning/expense report yourself to file your taxes or pass it along to an accountant to do it for you.

Making It Work for You

What's nice about being in charge is that you can make this whole endeavor work for you. You can take it as far as you want to go. Your handmade business can be a part-time job while you stay at home with your kids. It can be a full-time temporary job while you interview for jobs with your degree. Or it can be your full-time dream job that you turn into a profitable handmade business.

RESOURCES

ACCEPTING PAYMENTS

payments.intuit.com

paypal.com

squareup.com

BLOGGING TOOLS

blogger.com

squarespace.com

tumblr.com

typepad.com

wordpress.com

BOOKS

Sewing and quilting

Adventures in Design by Joen Wolfrom

All-in-One Quilter's Reference Tool by Harriet Hargrave, Sharyn Craig, Alex Anderson, Liz Aneloski (includes helpful charts for figuring yardage and more)

Color Play by Joen Wolfrom

Colorific by Pam Goecke Dinndorf

Essential Sewing Reference Tool by Carla Hegeman Crim

A Field Guide to Fabric Design by Kim Kight

The Practical Guide to Patchwork by Elizabeth Hartman

The Quilter's Color Club by Christine Barnes

Quilter's Handy Guide to Supplies & More by Dawn Cameron-Dick

Studio Color Wheel by Joen Wolfrom

Ultimate 3-in-1 Color Tool, Updated 3rd Edition by Joen Wolfrom

Visual Coloring by Joen Wolfrom

Photography

Beyond Snapshots by Rachel Devine and Peta Mazey

DSLR Photography for Beginners by Brian Black

Photography for Bloggers eBook by Vanessa Hewell (lbgstudio.bigcartel.com > Products > Photography for Bloggers eBook)

Understanding Exposure by Bryan Peterson

BUSINESS CARDS AND POSTCARD PRINTING

moo.com

vistaprint.com

CUSTOM FABRIC DESIGN

spoonflower.com

fabricondemand.com

first2print.com

modernyardage.com

FINDING CRAFT SHOWS AND FESTIVALS

craftsfaironline.com
This website offers links to thousands of crafters' websites plus listings of craft shows and information about suppliers, publications, newsgroups, classes, software, and more.

festivalnet.com
This searchable database of 25,000 festivals, arts and crafts shows, and other events also offers information on products, services, and resources for artists and other vendors. Membership starts at $49 a year.

unanimouscraft.com
A directory of resources for crafters, artists, and independent business owners

INVENTORY SOFTWARE FOR SMALL BUSINESS

inflowinventory.com

fishbowlinventory.com

MAILING LIST AND E-NEWSLETTER SERVICES

mailchimp.com

constantcontact.com

MANAGING FINANCES

godaddy.com > All Products > Invoicing & Payments > Online Bookkeeping

paypal.com

quicken.intuit.com

ONLINE ART AND CRAFT MARKETPLACES AND INFORMATION ABOUT THEM

artfire.com

bigcartel.com

craftbizblog.com

ebay.com

en.dawanda.com

etsy.com

ezebee.com

goodsmiths.com

handmadeartists.com

supermarkethq.com/browse/everything

zibbet.com

Things change fast. Keep up to date on what's going on, especially in Internet sales and sites; follow blogs; use the online sales user communities.

ONLINE CRAFT CLASSES

craftsy.com

creativebug.com

PHOTOGRAPHY

Photo editing

Adobe Photoshop

Adobe Photoshop Elements

Photoshop

GIMP

Serif PhotoPlus

Paint.net

PixBuilder Studio

Photography equipment

Reflectors
CowboyStudio 24″ × 36″ 5-in-1 collapsible reflector disc kit with stand and silver/gold/black/white/diffuser photo reflector

NEEWER 60cm 22″ 5-in-1 light multiphoto collapsible reflector

Tripod
Ravelli APLT4 61″ lightweight aluminum tripod with bag

Remote
Pixel Pro digital and film camera 100m wireless shutter remote control release

Lenses
Consult with a reputable camera shop about which lenses will best meet your needs.

Light tent
CowboyStudio 30″ Top Open Photo Softbox light tent

Extra
Professor Kobre's Lightscoop, flash device

SHIPPING AND OFFICE SUPPLIES

uline.com

SOCIAL MEDIA MANAGEMENT APPLICATIONS

hootsuite.com

tweetdeck.com

socialoomph.com

spredfast.com

ABOUT THE AUTHOR

Virginia Lindsay is a self-taught sewist and lover of all things fabric. She is the author of the popular sewing blog *Gingercake* and the designer behind the PDF pattern shop Gingercake Patterns and Design. She designs sewing patterns, several of which have been published by Simplicity. Her sewn items have been sold at many craft shows and her online shop, gingercakesews.etsy.com.

Virginia is a mother of four and is happily married to her husband, Travis. She lives outside of Pittsburgh in Freeport, Pennsylvania. Her kids inspire her every day, and she spends a lot of time playing cards, watching soccer, throwing baseballs, and listening to piano practice. When she is not taking care of her big family, you will find her taking walks outside, vegetable gardening, and sewing away in her home sewing studio.

Learn more about Virginia at gingercake.org.

stashBOOKS®

fabric arts for a handmade lifestyle

If you're craving beautiful authenticity in a time of mass-production...Stash Books is for you. Stash Books is a line of how-to books celebrating fabric arts for a handmade lifestyle. Backed by C&T Publishing's solid reputation for quality, Stash Books will inspire you with contemporary designs, clear and simple instructions, and engaging photography.

ctpub.com